Through The Years

Connecting Present to Past

Edited by
Cal McDonald & Gerald Richards

Book & Cover Design by Jonathan Gould

All letters by pupils
of Broughton High School and their pen pals.

An original work unleashed by the Super Power Agency, 2019.

superpoweragency.com

Introduction

by Gerald Richards, C.E.O of The Superpower Agency

In my initial talk with Broughton High School's Head of English, Nicola Daniel, I asked what the pupils in Mr. Brown's class would be working on during the term. She said one of the goals was to have the pupils learn and think about people other than themselves and with that vision the intergenerational pen pals project was born. We thought that connecting the pupils of Mr. Brown's class with older people in their community through the art of letter writing would be a great way for them to get to know another person, especially someone vastly different. Where did that person grow up? What was the world like when they were young? What did they do for fun?

This project, an effort to connect generations, young and old, has been a passion project of mine for quite some time. My great-grandmother passed away at the age of 100 when I was fourteen (and I was fourteen 36 years ago!). One of my biggest regrets was never being able to ask her what the world was like when she was young and who she wanted to be. Working with the pupils as they wrote their letters and watching them receive their responses from their pen pals was for me, and I think all the volunteers and staff, a sheer joy. Remember that excitement you had when you received a letter in the post? That was what every adult involved in the project got to see on our young people's faces on letter reception Friday. The Big Meet, where the pen pals met for the first time was truly one of the highlights of my career. Watching the care and attentiveness the young writers gave to their new friends was truly amazing. I don't think there was a dry eye in the house.

There are so many people to thank for making this project a reality but mostly I want to thank Mr. Brown and his pupils for sharing his classroom with us and our elder VIPs for being willing to share their life stories with their young pen pals. Magic can happen when you bring people together and this book is a prime example of the magic the Super Power Agency tries to bring to the lives of young people every day. Enjoy!

Foreword

by Mr Rory Brown, English Teacher, Brougthon High School

When the Pen Pals project was announced, I was a bit sceptical. How could we get a class who I had battled with all year to do small pieces of work to suddenly, and willingly, want to write? The idea for the project was to take some young, reluctant writers and give them an opportunity to connect with people they would normally never have the chance to interact with through the medium of letter writing. My 2Y4 class were those reluctant writers. They are an energetic class with a mixture of cultures, interests and ideas but they had one main thing in common – they all really didn't like writing.

Enter the Super Power Agency. Led by Gerald and Cal they brought in a group of volunteers from all over the world into my classroom to work with my class. Their enthusiasm and energy was palpable and before long, the pupils began to feel it as well. Suddenly, Brodie was furiously typing, asking questions about the life of his VIP and who his favourite football team was. Zander had begun to tell the stories of his chickens and Ella was musing about what her Pen Pal might be like. A once reluctant class had become excited, engaged writers in the space of a few weeks. Every Friday, the school library became a hive of activity. Volunteers and teachers moving from pupil to pupil answering their hundreds of questions about what to include in their first letter.

I will never forget the day my pupils opened their first letters. The look on their faces and the sheer joy and excitement as they called left and right to share what they had learned. It was clear that these kids had never had something like this before. They had never received a letter – never mind a beautifully hand written one that sometimes spanned several pages. Hilarity ensued when Callum was convinced his pen pal had been kidnapped when he was younger, when in reality he just loved the novel *Kidnapped*. So caught up and excited to read his letter, he sped through it and missed half of the details first time around.

One thing that struck me was just how much these unlikely pen pals had in common and this really came across when they finally met. Brodie and his pen pal, Geoff looked like two lifelong friends, chatting away as if they had not seen each other in years. Oliver and his pen pal Irene chatted and giggled conspiratorially about whether they wanted to be interviewed, and Hilari beamed throughout the afternoon. Cal and Gerald told me after that they had a number of things planned for that afternoon to fill the time, but in reality, it was never needed. It was amazing to watch the pupils' eyes light up as they interacted in person. Quiet pupils, who rarely spoke in class, were all of a sudden giggling and chatting away as if they had known their pen pals their whole lives.

Overall, this project has changed those pupils. I think they see the world a bit differently now and it will be something that they, and I, will never forget.

Mary & Zander

Letter 1 - Zander to Mary

Dear VIP,

My name is Zander, I am fourteen years old. I like nearly every kind of food and I'm not fussy. I've been to a lot of countries for holidays like: Germany, USA, UK and United Arab Emirates.

I just live with my mum and five chickens and two dogs. The dogs are two Staffordshire Bull Terriers called Chunk and Baxter. The five chickens are called: Tiffany, Rose, Pickle, Avatar and Nugget.

I really like cars, my favourite car is a Lamborghini Huracán LP-580. My favourite movie is Need For Speed and my favourite show is Scorpion.

I have a really cool Lego collection and by the way I went to Broughton High School, well I still go there.

Before my dad passed away he was running his own business called Gaulhofer Triple Glazing Windows. Now my mum runs the business.

It was nice writing to you and I would love to know some stuff about you. Thanks for being my pen pal.

Kind regards,

Zander

Dear Zander,

Thank you so much for taking so much care with writing your letter to me. I am delighted to be your pen pal. Your letter was very interesting, well done. I am amazed that you have visited so many countries already.

Ian, a friend of mine, kindly showed me a picture of your favourite car and I was very impressed. Ian also knew about your favourite movie Need For Speed and your favourite show 'Scorpion'.

Let me introduce myself -

I am a grandmother of two. Greg, my grandson, is aged thirteen. So like you, he is growing up fast. They live in Haddington, East Lothian, and I live near the Hibs football ground in Edinburgh.

I love animals. A neighbour has an elderly Staffy who likes to sit on my feet so that I can't move! Therefore I can only talk to the dog and make a fuss of him - the dog that is, not make a fuss of the neighbour - well maybe a little chat to the neighbour, if the dog allows.

I was sorry to hear that your dad passed away and your mum has stepped in to run the Gaulhofer Triple Glazing Windows business. My own dad was killed at sea before we ever met. He was serving in the Indian Ocean when his ship went down. I never saw him.

Although I never played with Lego, I loved making up anything from a friend's Meccano set, for hours.

Girls were not allowed to play with Meccano sets so I just borrowed my friend's set! Also I loved trains and still enjoy being in a train. On one occasion I was given an opportunity of helping to stoke up the fire boiler of a steam train with coal. It was hot work and hard work but I especially enjoyed it because girls normally were NEVER allowed to do this. I was allowed because I was a volunteer, unpaid, member of staff, so exempt from some rules, but careful with safety.

At present, I work as a volunteer helper at the LifeCare Centre, helping senior people to enjoy their time together. Also I help out with serving their lunches. We laugh a lot. On another day, I volunteer at the Mums and Toddlers group.

Like you, I enjoy my food, and I love to have a picnic outside. I like being in the countryside or the disused railways paths and enjoy a picnic there, and chat to the dogs as they pass by when my picnic is over.

Your chickens have great names. Do they like to follow you around? Sometimes I like to visit the Gorgie City Farm and be with the animals. Greg, my grandson, loved handling the one-day chicks. He was very very gentle, and was supervised by a member of their staff. Well, Zander it has been great writing to you, "the man of the house" helping your mum. She must be very proud of you. Take care, and I hope to hear from you again soon.

Best wishes - cheers,

from Mary

....

Letter 3 – Zander to Mary

Dear Mary,

Thank you so much for telling me about yourself and how it was when you were small.

I'm so sorry to hear about your dad that died while he was serving, God bless you.

Staffies are the best dogs, but chickens are the best overall.

What would you change if you were younger?

I'm sorry I didn't write a lot. I'll write more next time.

Kind regards,

Zander

....

Letter 4 – Mary to Zander

Dear Zander,

Many thanks for your letter. It was really good hearing from you. The fact that your letter was a little shorter did not matter to me at all. I just appreciated your very kind letter.

I am glad to learn that you have a special bond with your pets, and particularly so with your chickens Tiffany, Rose, Pickle, Avatar, and not forgetting Nugget. You mentioned that you thought that the chickens "are the best". I rather think that the chickens think that you are "the best".

It is amazing just how much pleasure our pets can give us as we care for their daily needs and spend quality time with them. They do not mind at all if we are fat or thin, tall or small, and whether or not we have the latest gadget or trainers. They just accept us the way we are.

Zander, in your last letter you wrote "what would you change if you were younger?" To be honest, I am not quite sure what you really meant but I will do my best to give you my thoughts. Please let me know if you think that I have misunderstood your question and I will try again and rephrase my reply.

I think that it is more difficult for a young person to have the authority to change some situations. In that case, a young person may be helped by sharing his concerns with someone he respects and who he feels he can trust. The more experienced person may be able to help and therefore improve the situation.

Many can be inspired by reading stories of great achievers. Many achievers, most actually, have had many failures and setbacks before success.

Speaking personally, some years ago I wanted to tour the north of Scotland very much. Many scoffed and ridiculed. I did not argue, but joined a cycle club. I learned a lot from the experienced cyclists, increased my cycling miles steadily and eventually I had a great holiday with my daughter Helen, cycling round the coast of the north of Scotland!

I do hope that you are enjoying school. Do you have any favourite subjects? Also do you have any thoughts on what you would like to do in the future? Whatever you decide, I do hope that all will go well for you. May you be able to buy your favourite car and treat your mum taking her somewhere nice. All the best to you, and thank you for being my pen pal.

Kind regards and best wishes,

Mary

Letter 5 - Zander to Mary

Dear Mary,

Thank you for writing back to me, I really appreciate the letter. You are right animals are the best, they keep you warm and give you company.

My favourite subject is maths. I love it and hope to get an A on the upcoming test next week. When I'm older I want to be an architect, it's really fun drawing houses and it's a well paid job. I also like CDT (Craft, Design, Technology).

I really like cycling and cycle every day to school. I love school, it's amazing. I hope you enjoy this letter, can't wait to read your reply and by the way your answer was really nice.

Kind regards,

Zander

Letter 6 Mary to Zander

Dear Zander

Thank you for your previous letter. I enjoyed reading your letter and I feel that I know you a little bit better.

I do hope that your maths test was successful and that you are delighted with the results.

You mentioned that you wish to become an architect when you are older. In addition, you asked me if I knew any architects. You also requested advice about architecture. At present, I do not know any architects. Although I am not qualified to give anyone career advice, I will gladly offer some basic suggestions based on my own experience.

Some years ago I loved working with a number of architects as their typist. I found the work very varied and interesting. It was also challenging and hard work. All the architects achieved very good certificates at school before completing their studies at University. It takes many years of dedicated study to qualify as an architect as the examinations are very difficult.

You have already indicated that you have a "really cool lego collection" and that you enjoy craft design and technology. In addition you mentioned that you like observing buildings. All these facts seem to indicate to me that you already have a passion for design & buildings.

Having a genuine passion for any career is very important, not only for ourselves but also for the clients and fellow workers. When we are enthusiastic about our work it is pleasant for everyone and clients want to come back.

I think that you are wise to continue doing your very best at school and continue to observe many varied designs and buildings. In this way you may prevent a problem.

For example, some public transports are fitted with seats which have fixed moulded headrest. This design is excellent for an average size person. For the tall or small person, the fixed moulded headrest may cause a sore back or a sore neck; not very much appreciated.

Thank you for being my pen pal. I do hope that we will be able to meet each other, perhaps sometime next year. In the meantime, may I wish you and your mum, not forgetting your dogs and chickens a lovely Christmas break. Our family will be attending special Christmas services, followed with Christmas pies.

All the best for you for 2019.

Kindest regards to all,

Mary

Tamsin & Ollie

Dear VIP,

My name is Tasnim and I am twelve years old. I was born in Syria but one year ago I moved to Edinburgh. I live with my Mum and Dad, and my sister and two brothers. The weather in Syria is sometimes sunny but it does snow sometimes too. My favourite food is fish and chips. I don't like pasta. My favourite film is The Little Mermaid. I love the songs and I wish I could swim in the ocean too. I have just moved to Broughton High School, I've only been here two days but so far it's going well.

I have three friends, Sidra, Rawaa and Hiba, I miss them. We all used to play basketball together on the school team. It's my favourite sport. My favourite book is Cinderella, I like the scary evil stepmother.

When I grow up I want to be a doctor. I like studying maths. I find it easy.

What is your job? What is your favourite food? What is your favourite book?

I'm excited to read your letter.

From,

Tasnim

Letter 2 - Ollie to Tasnim

Hi Tasnim,

Thank you for writing to me.

My name is Ollie and I live in Edinburgh, near Stockbridge. I am seventy-nine now and have lived in Scotland all my life.

I have worked a couple of jobs in my life. I used to be a typesetter, a job which doesn't exist any more. We used to arrange individual letters, one by one, to make up a whole printed page. I worked on making the train timetable posters, which involved a lot of tiny little letters and numbers to set. I also worked in satellite communication for a while.

My favourite book is probably 'Kidnapped' by Robert Louis Stevenson. I didn't play basketball much but really enjoyed football.

I am glad you are enjoying Broughton High. My sister used to go to the old Broughton High, but I did not. My favourite food is anything Italian.

I did not know Syria was snowy sometimes, that's very interesting! Are you enjoying being in Edinburgh? You should go for a walk up Princes Street and see the sights!

All the best,

Ollie

....

Letter 3 - Tasnim to Ollie

Dear Ollie,

Thank you for your lovely letter. I did not know that was a job. It must have taken you a very long time to set out all those individual letters.

My favourite Italian food is pizza, I like cheese, tomato and mushroom as my toppings! Did you ever play on a football team? Do you support a local team? You said you liked other sports - what other sports did you play?

I wouldn't like to work in satellite communication because I'm determined to be a doctor. I want to be able to help people who are sick. On a Friday afternoon I go to Edinburgh University to study Maths with other Arabic speakers, we study in English, but it's important for me to pass my exam in this subject. I enjoy studying at the university.

I am enjoying living in Edinburgh. I recently went to Princes Street and saw the

Christmas Market and the funfair rides, but I didn't go on any of them!

I am enjoying the new experience at Broughton High School. It's interesting that your sister went here too, I bet it's changed a lot since then. How many siblings do you have?

Do you enjoy watching films? If so, what's your favourite film?

Yours sincerely,

Tasnim M

....

Letter 4 - Ollie to Tasnim

Dear Tasnim,

Thanks for your letter, I've never had a pen pal before!

It's nice that you've seen the market, with all the lights and rides - these funfair things can be pretty dangerous - a couple of years ago I saw one of the rides broken down with people stuck on it which can't have been nice!

Broughton High hasn't changed too much since my sister was there but I think the education programmes have changed quite a bit. It was just my sister and I, she was five years older than me and is eighty-four now!

You asked me about football - I played for Herriot Hill, I played inside right. I support Hearts. I mainly like football but I used to swim at Glenogle Baths - which I loved.

I do like watching movies, I especially like Indiana Jones, the first film. Have you seen it?

Being a doctor is a good profession to be in, it seems pretty hard and takes a long time but would be worth it in the end.

Best wishes,

Ollie

Rakib & Danny

Letter 1 - Rakib to Danny

Dear VIP,

My name is Rakib and I am thirteen years old. I am from Edinburgh, Scotland. My parents are from Bangladesh which is in Asia. I have one sister and her name is Airah. I have 16+ cousins. I have brown eyes, black hair and I am kind of short. I am a happy person.

My hobbies are video games, art and football. I support Barcelona and my favourite player is Messi. I really would like to go to Barcelona and play football.

My favourite food is tomato & garlic pasta. My favourite movies are Avengers: Infinity War and Captain America: Civil War. My favourite colour is blue and green.

Now there's some questions I want to ask you. So, Number 1: what was life like when you were at my age? Number 2: Do you have a pet? Number 3: What are your favourite hobbies? Number 4: What's your favourite sport? Number 5: Did you ever go on holidays?

I hope to hear from you.

Best Wishes,

Rakib

Dear Rakib,

Thank you so much for your letter, which I read with interest today.

My name is Danny, although I was given the name Dennis when I was born. I am eighty-eight years old and live in Edinburgh.

When I was your age I attended Holy Cross Academy in Edinburgh.

I used to do a milk round in the mornings, delivering milk to households. Then in the evening I worked as a delivery boy after school at a chemist shop.

When I was fourteen years old I then left school! Can you imagine leaving school at your age? That would be strange! I then joined the railway after passing an exam. It was around three years after World War II when I joined the RAF as part of the National Service at the age of eighteen years, for two years. I was based mainly in Glasgow.

It is interesting about your football. You must work hard and follow your dream if you want to be a footballer.

I was also interested in sport. I became an International Basketball referee when I was thirty-five years old. I refereed all ages from sixteen years to sixty years, teams from Scotland.

I travelled to England, Ireland, Wales as well as to Italy, France, USA and beyond! I was the manager of the Scottish International Senior Men's team. I went to the USA with the very first British Basketball team ever to compete in the USA. We were very excited to take part and went there for three weeks. We appeared on the Ed Sullivan Show. It was very exciting.

My profession was being a photographer and I took wedding and social photographs mainly at events etc. I was self-employed. There used to be something called a 'pour oot' or 'scatter' after a wedding. The best man would scatter lots of change into the crowd to cheer and for children to enjoy. I don't think they do that anymore. Have you heard of that before?

One of my favourite photographs that I took was when the tall ships came into Leith Docks. What an amazing spectacle!

I had two sisters, and my mum and dad. We all lived together in Stenhouse and then we moved to Leith.

I had ten cousins but they mainly lived in Fife so we didn't see them very often.

I had a pet dog.

I don't really have a favourite movie but I was also really keen on dancing. My wife and I competed in amateur dancing and appeared in the TV show called Come Dancing. My favourite dance was the slow foxtrot. On a Saturday night when I was young we used to go dancing to the Palais. That was a chance to get dressed up, and we loved it.

We used to go on holiday most years, and my family were the first to go on holiday to Spain in 1963. Franco was in charge of the country then.

Are you part of a football team and do they have teams at school that compete? Or is that when you are a bit older?

You mention also that you are interested in art? Are you good at drawing?

It had been lovely to write to you and I look forward to hearing from you again soon.

Yours sincerely,

Danny

....

Letter 3 - Rakib to Danny

Dear Danny,

I read your letter and I have learned a lot about you. It was quite surprising that you left school at the age of fourteen and you joined the RAF for two years! It was cool how you travelled to England, Ireland, Wales, Italy, France and USA. You've been on many TV shows and it is very exciting. I really like taking photos but I will never be as good as you. It was really good that you passed an exam.

I'm not part of a football team but hopefully in the future I will be part of a football team. I really like art and I actually won the School Arts 2018 Award. I am really good at drawing, especially sketching.

Now it's my turn to ask tons of questions.

1. What was your favourite basketball team?

2. Do you still live with your wife?

3. Was it hard milk rounding in the morning?

4. Have you been a photographer or are you still one?

5. What advice to you wish you'd been given at my age and why?

It was cool to write to you and read your letter, I am also looking forward to hearing from you again.

Yours Sincerely,

Rakib

Dear Rakib,

Delighted to receive your reply and congratulations on winning the school's Arts 2018 award.

In answer to your questions: -

1. My favourite American basketball team was the Boston Celtics. I saw them twice when I was in America. My favourite European team was Yugoslavia (which does not exist now of course) which I refereed at the pre-Olympic games in Edinburgh 1972. They were a lovely group of guys, very professional and true sportsmen. My favourite Scottish team was 'Murray International Metals' - sponsored by David Murray. I refereed many matches (two or three per season, over ten seasons).

2. I am afraid my wife died in 1999. My son is sixty-two years, and I have two daughters in their fifties (one lives in Australia). I am going to visit my daughter on Christmas day.

3. My milk round was based in Leith. I started at 6.30am and finished at around 8am.

I had to transport approx one-hundred bottles of milk up and down the streets and stairs. It was very hard work. I think I earned around 20p a day.

I thought it would be interesting for you to know a little about the currency back then:

1 Farthing = 1/4 of an old pence

1 Sixpence = 2.5p decimal money (6d old money)

1 Shilling = 12p (12d old money)

1 Thrupenny = ½ sixpence

20 shillings in one pound (old money)

Half crown = 2/6 (2 shillings, six pence) (old money)

I am no longer a professional photographer as I retired at age sixty-five years.

My advice to you would be to work hard at school and take up a sport which you enjoy and always to persevere.

Be good to your parents and your relatives and friends. Stay out of trouble and do your best at school.

All the very best and I look forward to meeting you next week.

Best wishes,

Danny

....

Letter 5 - Rakib to Danny

Dear Danny,

I read your reply and thank you for answering my questions. I have learned a lot from you and I am happy for you that you are visiting your daughter (especially on Christmas Day). It is sad to hear your wife is no longer with us but wherever you go she will always see you. It's pretty cool to hear that your daughter lives in Australia. Wow! Transporting one-hundred milk bottles! (Yeah that is pretty hard!)

Currency was pretty interesting, I liked it. I am surprised that you have played a lot of sport, I guess you were a good referee. Ok, I have some questions for you:

1. Do you like art?
2. Who was your favorite football player?
3. Are you doing anything special on Christmas? (apart from visiting your daughter).

Ok, now my last question is, what's your favourite food?

Ok, now thank you for replying and I really like your letter, hopefully I will be meeting you soon. I am really excited.

Yours Sincerely,

Rakib

Dear Rakib,

Thank you for your latest letter,

Yes I am looking forward to Christmas and spending it with my family. It is amazing to think it is just around the corner now.

You asked me in your letter if I enjoyed art. I am more interested in music. I enjoy popular and light classical music. I have been to the Queens Hall in Edinburgh a few times and enjoyed light orchestra music.

My favourite artist is Al Jolson. He was an incredible artist. I also enjoy Michael Bublé and Dean Martin from the Rat Pack era.

Regarding football - I liked Gordon Smith, who played for Hibs, he was one of the 'Famous Five'.

I will be attending the Christmas Party at LifeCare. It is always nice and we enjoy entertainment and turkey for lunch! My favourite food is cottage pie and I like clootie dumpling.

When I was young we used to put a silver thruppenny inside the Christmas pudding! Always exciting as a child to see if you could find it in your pudding.

I hope you have a lovely Christmas. I look forward to meeting you in soon.

With best wishes,

From Danny

Irene & Oliver

Letter 1 - Oliver to Irene

Dear VIP,

Hello my name is Oliver and I am thirteen years old and I was born in 2005. I have two brothers and a mum and dad and I play a game called Fortnite. It is a video game. I could be playing it all day and you kill people to get a victory royale and you can get skins. My hobbies are I play rugby and sometimes play football.

I was in Orlando this year and the flight was eleven to twelve hours for two flights/planes and last year I went to Majorca for a week and it was very good. Have you been to any good holidays?

I have two cats called Elay & Daisy. I used to have a dog called Ruben but me and dad sold him.

What was it like when you were little?

From best wishes,

Oliver

Letter 2 - Irene to Oliver

Dear Oliver,

Nice to hear from you. My name is Irene and I was born in 1928. I came to Edinburgh from Aberdeen six years ago.

I have one brother - three sons - three grandsons - three granddaughters and two great grandsons. Do you have grandparents? I have one grandson living in Edinburgh. The rest of my grandkids are living elsewhere.
I used to have a cat, she was called Heidi. She got that name because she was always hiding. I didn't have a pet when I was growing up but my Grannie had a cat and his job was to catch mice.
I played hockey when I was at school. I enjoy watching good games of rugby and football.
I have been to Majorca and New York and nearer to home in Dublin.
I have a mobile phone and I have a tablet and a computer. I enjoy a game of Scrabble.

I look forward to hearing from you again soon Oliver.

Bye for now,

Irene

....

Letter 3 - Oliver to Irene

Dear Irene,

Thank you for writing to me. I really enjoyed reading your letter.

I had a granny and a grandad but last year my grandad died. My granny lives around the corner. I also have a granny and grandad up at my dad's and they live in Tranent. I had a dog called Ruben because he eats everything he finds on the floor.
I have never played Scrabble and I am sure it would be good for my spelling, I might try and play it on my phone.
I am very impressed that you can use a phone and a tablet.
Did you find it easy to learn to use the computer?
We learn in school but I find things hard because I have dyslexia.
Thanks for reading my letter.
Hope to hear for you again.

Kind regards,

Oliver

Dear Oliver,

So good to hear from you again. I am pleased to know you are enjoying my letters and I hope you can read my writing. Handwriting has changed so much over the years.

I have not ever written a letter on my computer. It is so easy to use a phone or text a message or even email.

Many years ago I joined an Evening Class to learn about computers. Compared to today's standards it was basic, but difficult at the time.

We were taught alignment, save as, copy & paste and spreadsheets. I never used any of it. My age group at the time asked for too much explanation and we had to stop asking so many questions and get on with it. Computers in business premises were few and far between. I get Google to answer my questions now.

I forgot to say that I have one of my grandsons in Sydney, Australia and one in London. A granddaughter in Vancouver - one in Dublin and one in Aberdeen so we are pretty scattered.

Do you have plans for Xmas?

I have been invited to Aberdeen to be with family or I can be here in Edinburgh, I have not quite made of my mind yet. The weather is a bit daunting.

That seems to be all for now Oliver until next time.

Bye for now,

Irene

Letter 5 - Oliver to Irene

Dear Irene,

Happy St Andrew's Day!

Will you be eating haggis?

I can read your writing very well. We do lots of handwriting at school but the computers are easier than written work.

It is so good that you have family all over the world and it sounds exciting. Have you ever been to see them? It must take a long time to travel to see them.

Did you ever travel by boat or in a plane? Do they ever travel to see you in Scotland?

I have nothing planned for Christmas apart for going out for dinner. I really like roast turkey. I don't like brussel sprouts! Do you like them? I can make mince pies and I enjoy baking.

I think it is nice to be with family at Christmas but I hope you make the right choice for you.

Bye for now,

Oliver

Kate & Tom

Dear VIP,

Hello my name is Kate, and I'm thirteen years old and I live in Edinburgh. I live with my mum, dad and brother. Half of my family is American. My hobbies are swimming, shopping, photography and cycling. I'm generally a nice person. I can be shy with meeting new people but I'm kind and outgoing.

I have two cats called Noah and Alfie they are brothers and they are one and a half years old. They are ragdoll cats so they sleep a lot and are fairly lazy but when the toys come out they are very playful. I also have a fish which is five years old. I used to have six but they sadly passed away after the years. And even though I don't have any dogs they are my favourite animals and I hope to get one soon.

My favourite movies are Parent Trap and The Greatest Showman. What's yours?

In the future I would like to be an interior designer or an architect and if that dream fails then I'll try be a photographer because I love designing things and taking photos. What have your past jobs been and how were they?

I'm very excited to be learning about you. So I need to ask you some questions so let's get started - don't worry it won't be that much. I have never been out of the country but when I'm older I would love to travel the world. So I was wondering if you have been to any interesting places? If so, where was your favorite place that you have travelled and where do you recommend? I'm looking forward to meeting you.

Sincerely,

Kate

Dear Kate,

I was very impressed when I received your letter and for your age, I think it was exceptionally well written. My name is Tom, although my first name is really James! I am ninety years and ninety-one years in December 2018. I live alone. I have a daughter and a son.

My daughter lives in Wolverhampton and my son stays in Edinburgh. My daughter visits me every fortnight which I look forward to, I also have three grandchildren (two boys and a girl).

I look forward to visiting my grandsons in Wolverhampton at Christmas time.

My granddaughter is thirty years old and she designs stage sets for theatre, and she lives in London, she works all over the world and has a very creative job, which she really loves. My grandson studies at Edinburgh University and received an Honours Degree in Geography and Engineering. He now works in London, but I think he may end up in Australia.

When I was young (from the age of seventeen years) I became interested in sport, particularly rugby. I played rugby for school (Trinity Academy) and continued playing with the Former Pupils' team. I love to watch rugby on TV, I even worked as a steward at Murrayfield when I was in my forties to sixties.

When I left school I worked for the Ordnance Survey who made maps. I was called up to the army for three years (1945-1949). There was no choice to join, I was eighteen years old. I was based in the survey department of The Royal Engineers and after six months training I was sent abroad to the Middle East and Kenya at the end of the war.

I really enjoyed visiting those countries and I loved to learn about new cultures and the people. I really enjoyed Kenya. It was a very simple life. I saw so many wonderful animals: zebras, elephants, giraffes, etc. When I came out of the army I became a surveyor. I worked all over Scotland for Scottish Special Housing and then Wimpey.

Going to the cinema was not really my interest but I used to love going dancing at the Plaza in Edinburgh - I used to go on a Wednesday, Friday and Saturday night during the 1950s and 1960s. I know how to do the Tango, quick step and the slow foxtrot!

You seem to be a very creative person. That is wonderful. It is important for you to know your dreams and to make them happen.

I am delighted to be able to correspond with you and I look forward to receiving your reply soon.

Yours sincerely,

Tom

Dear Tom,

It was really nice getting your reply and I was really interested by your letter. Thanks for writing back. I appreciated you saying that my letter was well written, I can tell you're a really kind man.

Reading about you being in the army really interested me. I would like to know more about what it was like. It must have been exciting traveling to all these different places. I was worried because you letter nearly got lost, but it's safe now.

It was cool knowing that you know how to do a few dances. I started dancing when I was three and I started with junior ballet and tap. Then when I was six I started doing dance competitions and when I was ten I moved on to do contemporary dance. I won lots of medals and trophies. I had to stop dancing when I was eleven because my mum wanted me to focus more on studies and not dance. I was quite upset at the time but whenever there is a chance to do a dance workshop at school then I'm the first one to zoom their hand up. Ha Ha.

It's nice how you look forward to seeing your grandson at Christmas time. I love Christmas. I like spending time with my friends and family. On Christmas day I spend it with my family but a few days before me and my friends have a tradition when we do something fun to celebrate the Christmas holidays. This year it's a sleep over at my house with my six best friends. We are doing Secret Santa and watching movies. What is your traditional christmas like?

Yours sincerely,

Kate

....

Dear Kate,

Thank you for your letter, it was lovely to hear from you again.

I wanted to ask you have you decided what subjects you will choose to sit at S3? It is difficult to decide, do you know whether you might go down the creative route or not?

If you concentrate on your studies it opens up a whole new world to you. So many opportunities these days to travel with your job. To learn new things when you study, that will help you shape your future. You learn a great deal. When I was your age there was less opportunity. It is really about going with your heart and doing something you love and are interested in.

I was always interested in geography and maps.

In 1940, I was thirteen years old. World War II had already begun. I was evacuated with my two younger brothers to Winchburgh (a small mining village) with our mum and we stayed there for two years.

Rationing of food and clothing was difficult. We had coupons to buy sugar/butter etc. We were able to get meat, but fruit such as bananas was scarce.

When I was called up to the army I received three shillings a day. I was a surveyor in the army.

My job was to make sure that very important maps of the beach areas in France (where the war office would be planning the landings) were printed and then delivered to London. We had to keep the maps hidden. All very secretive! There were not so many women in the army then, they mainly joined the RAF.

You mentioned your love of dancing. With Strictly Come Dancing it has grown in popularity. I noticed music and dance are specialist areas at your school. It is important to concentrate on your studies like your mum says and there might be an opportunity in the future to explore dance again, or even to enjoy it as part of a show, etc?

My granddaughter, as I have mentioned before, started at the Glasgow School of Music and Dance (The Conservatoire). She studied music and drama. And she now travels the world of stage set design.

Christmas is always a family affair. When I was young I used to look forward to receiving a box of soldiers, a sixpence, an apple and orange. I am sure you will have a wonderful time with your friends and having the sleepover. Such fun!

We didn't have sleepovers, only gatherings of family when I was young.

What is on your Christmas list this year? I hope your wishes come true.

I look forward to meeting you when possible.

Yours sincerely,

Tom

Charlie & Kai

Dear VIP,

My name is Kai and I am fourteen and live in the Granton area. I really enjoy video games like Fornite. Do you like video games? I also like football, especially FC Barcelona. Do you like football?

From

Kai

....

Letter 2 - Charlie to Kai

Hello Kai,

I am sixty-eight years of age and was brought up in the Granton area. We lived overlooking Granton Harbour where we messed about in boats. My father was a good sailor and as a family we sailed from Granton to Aberdour at an early age (six months old).

When I was younger I played rugby for Ainslie Park School and scored several tries. When I left school I served my apprenticeship in a shipyard in Leith which lasted for four years. Afterwards I joined the Merchant Navy and sailed from Glasgow to Australia, on several occasions, with a cargo of boneless beef, butter and powdered milk.

I'm afraid I don't have any computer games at hand, but glad you'd like playing these games on your computer. The only games I played on the computer was golf courses around the world. I also enjoyed playing tennis, and swimming, and fishing, and horse riding. I liked to support the Scotland rugby team and go Murrayfield and see South Africa, New Zealand, Wales, beat Scotland on several occasions.

I hope you can read all of this and look forward to hearing from you in the coming weeks.

Yours faithfully,

Charlie

....

Letter 3 - Kai to Charlie

Dear Charlie,

I live in Granton as well. I also live overlooking the harbour. I've been to a Hibs game.

On the weekend I go to Pilton Park with my friends and play football. Sometimes we go to each other's houses and play FIFA. I would like to travel a lot as well.

Sometimes I go to the game shop with my dad and get the latest game.

Thank you for writing to me and I'm looking forward to hearing from you.

From,

Kai

Dear Kai,

Thank you for your letter. I was interested in the fact that you live in the Granton area of Edinburgh. I spent most of my childhood messing about in boats in Granton Harbour. I too used to travel via Pilton Park on my way to school, and watch the football although I am a rugby man myself and supported a local team, called Heriots of Goldenacre. When the game was finished we used to go for a pie and a pint next to the pavillion.

I am afraid I haven't much experience in computer games at all but glad you are able to go to the games shop with your dad. How much pocket money do you get, or do you rent the games?

My main form of exercise comes from exercising my Lakeland Terrier, so I have seen many parks, and wasteland. Hope you are well.

Take care,

Charlie

Hilari & Ian

Letter 1 - Hilari to Ian

Dear VIP,

My name is Hilari and I'm twelve years old and I live in Edinburgh. But at home my family and most of my friends call me Jessica. I was raised in Portugal and I moved here to Edinburgh when I was eight.

I live with my two older brothers and my mum, and I have looooooooots of cousins and aunts. My favourite food is chicken nuggets and I love the smoothie from McDonalds and the McChicken Sandwich.

My favourite TV show is Riverdale, Vampire Diaries and Teen Wolf :)

What's your favourite food?

Where did you grow up?

What's your name?

What countries have you been to?

Do you have any siblings?

What do you like and not like?

What was your favourite holiday?

Do you like chicken nuggets?

I'm looking forward to hearing from you and hopefully meeting you

Best wishes,

Hilari

Letter 2 - Ian to Hilari

Dear Hilari,

Thank you for your letter, you have asked me lots of questions, I'll try to answer them.

I was born in Edinburgh in 1933, but have travelled over the world, from Singapore to Syria and France.

Now your questions, my favourite food is tapas (Spanish). I have a brother and a sister, younger than me. My favourite holidays are France and Spain, good food and good weather.

I do not eat chicken nuggets! But I enjoy chicken legs!

It would be great if we can meet up at a future visit, I would look forward to that.

Ian

P.S. Write again any time!

....

Letter 3 - Hilari to Ian

Dear Ian,

Thank you for your nice letter. I have a lot of questions!

What was Edinburgh like back then? I'm not sure what I'd like to do when I leave school yet. What was France like? Can you speak any French?

My favourite TV programme is Riverdale - it's about teenagers. What did you like to do when you were a teenager?

What's your favourite food? What are you going to do for Christmas? What did you and your family like to do back in 1933?

I have two big brothers and my older brother is good and the second brother loves to tease me. Did you fight with your brother and sister? Were you married and do you have any kids? When school break comes I'm going out with my friend and family and going to the cinemas with my friends.

It would be lovely to meet you.

Love, Hilari

Dear Hilari,

Thanks for replying to my letter, I'll try to answer your questions.

Remember I was born in 1933, I don't know much about that time. I was at Primary School during the 1939-1945 war. The war didn't really affect us in Edinburgh a great deal, although my Gran McLaren had an unexploded bomb near her house in Edinburgh. There were trams and buses in Edinburgh when I was at school. My family didn't have a car, in fact cars were very rarely something most people had.

France is a lovely country and French people like to hear you try to talk their language even if you make mistakes! My French is not too good.

I will be with my family at Christmas, my son and his wife and my grandchildren, both grown up.

I have no brothers or sisters, unfortunately they both died a few years ago. I think lots of siblings have arguments but I was much older than my brother and sister.

Sorry about my writing but I have cramp in my hand.

Have a lovely Christmas, I am looking forward to meeting you.

Regards,

Ian

Grace & Jan

Letter 1 - Grace to Jan

Dear VIP

Hello my name is Grace. I am thirteen years old I live in Edinburgh I live with my mum, dad and four big brothers. My favorite food is chips and a cheeseburger from McDonalds with a Irn Bru. I love tomato sauce. I basically eat it with everything. I hate brown sauce except from the chippy, that's amazing. My favorite movie is The Grinch during Christmas season and I like Mr Bean. I hate scary movies but I still watch them a lot. Can you tell me some facts about you now please?

My hobbies are going swimming and going ice skating. I have done a lot of dancing and gymnastics. I stopped doing it four years ago but I am starting back up for Edinburgh Dance Academy. I love hanging out with my friends and chilling on the weekend. I have a season ticket for Hibs at Easter Road. What are your favorite hobbies?

I have been to Spain a lot with my family. I love going on planes - they are fun and I like meeting pals on holiday. I have been to Gran Canaria, Majorca and Benidorm twice. When I was younger I always went to a caravan but now I go abroad. What holidays have you been on or want to go on? I really want to go to America and Disneyland in Paris. I am going in two years with my best friend and about twenty other people.

I spend most of my time on my phone and I am always on Snapchat on social media. Do you have a phone, laptops or an iPad? When I leave school I want to be a makeup artist or a lawyer.

What was your job? I look forward to hearing about my VIP and hopefully meeting you one day.

Best wishes, Grace

Dear Grace,

Thank you so much for your letter which I enjoyed reading. My name is Jan and although I too live in Edinburgh, I am much older than you!

You are lucky to have four big brothers and I hope they look after you? My older brother sadly died in a car accident many years ago when he was working in South Africa - he had a very interesting and happy life but I will always miss him a little bit.

Good for you for enjoying swimming! Not only is it important for safety but really healthy. I am happier swimming in the sea than in swimming pools as I don't like chlorine or bumping into people! (and am no longer very good at it and prefer to swim on my back).

Good luck with the Edinburgh Dance Academy, why did you stop dancing four years ago? I have to confess I have never drunk Irn Bru or been to a football match!! - but I did once have a boyfriend who was the nephew of the man who owned Hibs! But I don't suppose that counts?

My hobbies have been walking in the hills, watching birds through binoculars and playing the violin. I have done a lot of travelling abroad in the past and worked overseas as a nurse which was amazing. I too have been to Majorca and it is a beautiful island - I once climbed down a river gorge with sides so close you could touch them both and was a bit scared in case there was a storm and water came crashing down!

Regarding food - I like it all!!! And agree with you over tomato sauce and chips! However as I now work as a volunteer in the Botanic Gardens I also really enjoy eating vegetables (which we grow) and the potatoes for the chips, which we grow also. Some schools have small plots and come during the summer to grow and cook things in the Botanic Cottage.

Yes, I have a laptop, iPad and phone but live in a different world from you!! I use my laptop mostly for email, looking things up and to keep in touch with what's going on... but I do not use social media as for me it could create pressure and possibly be stressful!!

When we went on a night out in my youth we made an arrangement to meet beforehand and kept to it. I believe these days you constantly keep in touch with your phones and meet up at the last minute?

I once took a year with friends to drive across Africa. There were no such things as mobile phones and we had to write letters home which we posted in big cities along the route. We picked up the replies in the next city further along and sometimes it took a month each way for the letters! So our news was mostly out of date but always very exciting to receive. It did not seem strange or dangerous; it was the way things were then... and to me it does not seem that long ago!

You asked me what was my job - I was a nurse and midwife most of my life which I thoroughly enjoyed.

Perhaps you could tell me what your favourite lessons are at school and who are the people you intend to go to America and Paris with in two years time? Are they a group from school? Do you like animals and do you have any pets?

I hope this is what you wanted to know and I look forward to hearing from you again.

All the best,

From Jan

....

Letter 3 - Grace to Jan

Dear Jan,

Thank you so much for your lovely letter. I know never ask a lady your age but how old are you Jan? You seem to be very active swimming on your back! And volunteering for the Botanic Gardens. In fact I am going there this evening for a Christmas light show. What job do you do at the gardens?

I gave up Edinburgh Dance Academy because it took up a lot of my time and I couldn't go out with my friends cause I had dance. Now I miss it! I will try vegetables if you try some Irn Bru.

You will have to tell me what vegetables I will like?

Besides Africa have you travelled anywhere else as you seem to like adventure?

As a midwife how many babies have you delivered and have you seen any of them growing up?

My favorite lessons are Art, PE, English and Drama. I am going to America with my best friend and her mum, dad and sister with about twenty other of our friends.

I love animals. I have fish, about fifteen. I really would love a dog though!

Sorry to hear that you lost your brother. My brothers are called Scott, Ross, James and Ben and they look after me very well. Do you have any other siblings and have you ever had any other pets?

I look forward to hearing from you and have a nice week.

Best wishes,

Grace

....

Letter 4 - Jan to Grace

Hi Grace,

Many thanks for your reply... I shall tell you my age when we meet!

Although I do volunteer in the Botanic Gardens and various other things - the swimming on my back was more of a statement 'what I would do' if I still went swimming!!!

I totally understand why you gave up dance - it is exactly the same reason I gave up playing the violin - but it is never too late to start again and I think you won't regret it.

There is no way I can tell you what vegetables you would like! We all have different tastes, sometimes it is the way they are cooked - but I really like green vegetables such as broccoli cooked with a bit of butter and pepper. There is a shop in Stockbridge next to the post office which sells great big carrots with soil still on and they are more delicious than any from the supermarket!!

However when I was young I really hated vegetables! I think our tastes change as we get older as I'm almost vegetarian now. In my school days no one left at lunch time and we all ate a hot meal cooked in the school. Of course we complained about everything but looking back some were really good! All schools throughout the country cooked the same and the apple crumble with custard was actually delicious!

As a midwife I delivered fifty-two babies but no, I have no idea where any of them are now. I was working in the Lake District at the time and my contract lasted only until the eleventh day.

However, as an ex-Health Visitor in Edinburgh I still bump into children who were 'mine' and now in their twenties, thirties! - older than you!

I'm glad you like animals and I too have fish, which need more looking after than you would imagine! In the past I have kept tortoises, guinea-pigs and a rescue cat called Esme who was my best friend for sixteen years. Dogs are lovely but they need a lot of care, love and money to look after them properly, perhaps best to wait a bit…

I hope you liked the lights at the Botanic Gardens, I would be most interested to hear your thoughts!

I promise to buy and try a bottle of Irn Bru before we meet!

Take care and I look forward to hearing from you.

Jan x

Femi & Allan

Letter 1 - Femi to Allan

Dear VIP,

My name is Femi and I am thirteen years old and my birthday is in November. My hobbies are football, basketball and cycling. I have a mum and a dad, two brothers and three sisters. My cousin is a pro-boxer. I have been to Hastings, Newcastle, Nigeria, Holland. Where have you been?

In my spare time I like to go out with my friends. What did you like to do in your spare time? What was it like at school when you were my age?

What was your greatest memory? Do have any kids? Have you been on any holidays? What was your dream job when you where a kid?

The football teams I support are Hearts and Liverpool.

Best of wishes,

from Femi

Dear Femi,

I was really pleased to get your letter. Thank you for writing.

My name is Allan. I'm sixty-four years old and I work at BBC Scotland - on their Arts website, actually. We write articles and make short films on painters, musicians, actors, dancers and filmmakers. It is interesting and I know I'm lucky to be doing this. I've worked there for about thirty years. I used to make Arts documentaries before working online.

I'm married to Susan and we have one son, Teo, who is twenty. When I'm feeling old and creaky and I chat to Teo, I feel younger and more enthusiastic, because he's very positive! I like the fact you have so many brothers and sisters. I have one sister, who is seven years older than I am. We're close now that we're adults but when I was young, seven years was quite a gap. With all those brothers and sisters, was yours a noisy house? Did you all get on well together?

Because my Dad changed jobs a few times, I changed school quite often. It meant I had to leave friends behind and the schools could be quite different. Once, I moved from a boarding school where - every day - I'd do thirty minutes homework before breakfast, then study all morning, have lunch, play a game of rugby or run three or four miles, then have a few more lessons before tea. This was followed by more homework, then bed. I moved from that strict school to another, where I was taught by Catholic priests - and you could walk out of the school gates anytime and no one would stop you!

Do you enjoy school? I guess sometimes it can be a pain but you'll have friends there and I think most teachers try their best. I was an English teacher for three years at Boroughmuir after I left University. I didn't know what I wanted to do and I thought teachers had long holidays! I couldn't believe how hard we had to work; teaching, marking, planning new lessons - and giving up our Saturday mornings for sports. I came away really respecting them.

I was attracted by your name, Femi. That's a great name. I've just been working with someone called Femi. He was born in Nigeria but brought up in London. He seemed a really gentle, sweet guy but as a teenager got into a bit of trouble. But he discovered music and took up the guitar - it turned his life around. He found what he loved. He's now a successful guitarist and has played with lots of successful musicians, like Amy Winehouse. He wrote and filmed a beautiful song for us, called "Alafia" which in the Yoruba language means "peace". I saw that you'd travelled to Nigeria - why was that? I think Femi might be a shorter version of Olufemi. Is that your full name?

I see you've been travelling - what's your favourite place so far - and why? I've been really lucky because of my job. I've been able to travel to New York, Los Angeles and quite a few European cities. It's always exciting travelling somewhere new; I really enjoy it. Do you?

I'm not sure I've answered all your questions - but I'll be writing again soon. You asked me what my greatest memory was. That's a powerful thought. I'll have to consider that for next time. What was yours? I'm keen to hear more about the things you enjoy and why. These are the things that keep you going.

Until then, all the very best,

Allan

....

Letter 3 - Femi to Allan

Dear Allan

I loved your letter thanks for writing back . I have a question for you, the guy called Femi how did he get in trouble when he was a teenager? I guess it's time for to answer some questions. My full name is not Olufemi, it's Obafemi but my brother's name is Olutobi.

You asked asked me if I have a noisy house it's kind of noisy but not too loud but we all get along. I have a question for you would rather go to rather go to school in your time or now?

That's all I have got to say.

All the very best,

Femi

....

Letter 4 - Allan to Femi

Dear Femi,

Thank you for your letter. You asked about Femi, the musician I was working with, about how he got into trouble as a teenager. I haven't talked directly with him about this but he has spoken about it elsewhere. He has mentioned it in connection with how he took up guitar; "It was a direct result of being a little bit wayward, getting into trouble, and my mum thinking the best way to keep an eye on me, especially on a Saturday evening, was to take me along to the church choir practice, where I discovered a couple of other young guys playing the guitar." That was his step-mum, as his birth mother died when he was very young. He left Nigeria for London when he was ten, which must have been quite a change for him, what was your reason for going to Nigeria?

Would I rather go to school now or when I did (the 1960s and 70s)? When I was at school most of the time it was very strict and you had much less freedom than you have now. I suppose I had less choice of things to do and likely less money to spend in the holidays. While teachers wanted you to do well, I suspect there was less pressure (and choice) than now; it was more straightforward. Sometimes, I think I'd find it difficult to survive as a teenager now. At worst, it feels like you have to make out you're doing exciting things all the time on social media, looking to be successful (or even famous!) and worrying about what your friends think of you.

I've probably got the wrong end of the stick - have I? - but with us, it seemed a little more innocent; some boredom, some mischief and do the best you can. Because you weren't expected to be amazing, it was easier. How do you feel about school and friends?

Nowadays, if I was a teenager, I'd want to find some friends I could trust, who didn't show off and no one felt they had anything to prove. Underneath, everyone's a bit uncertain about things and just want to be with pals who accept each other for who they are. Also no one's perfect. What do you think?

I'm pleased your (slightly noisy) family get on. The fact you've all grown up together is a very special kind of friendship. Hopefully you'll all look out for each other as you go through life.

Next time, tell me about your cycling!

My best wishes,

Allan

Dear Allan,

Thanks very much for your letters, I'm enjoying reading them very much.

That story about Femi was interesting. I went to Nigeria to visit my uncle. I really liked Nigeria, it was really hot. I was there for ten days living in a hotel. In the hotel the breakfast was so nice. For breakfast I had crêpes with strawberries and chocolate spread. And then we went to a waterpark with my uncle while my dad and mum went shopping.

I used to play the samba drums at a drum club but my football training days were on the same days as the samba drum days so I did my football instead because I liked it better.

You asked about my cycling I don't do any cycling clubs but I like to cycle to a lot of places. I had a mountain bike, it was blue but it has got too small for me so for Christmas I am getting a bigger mountain bike and it is called a Caliber. For Christmas some of my family are coming from Hastings to come and see us. I am looking forward to it.

Are you spending Christmas with family?

Wherever you are I hope you have a very happy Christmas.

Best wishes,

from Femi

Ella & Maureen

Letter 1 - Ella to Maureen

Dear VIP,

Hello my name is Ella and I am thirteen and I go to Broughton High School in Edinburgh and I am in S2. I am mostly a happy person and sometimes shy. I have brown straight hair and eyes.

I have a little sister called Gwen. She is eighteen months old and very cute with brown curly hair. I love to draw, take pictures, watch TV/YouTube and I play hockey on Fridays and swim on Tuesdays. What sports did you play as a kid?

I HATE spiders, even though they are so harmless. One time in camp there was a huge spider on the wall and my friends were so scared that they could not go to bed soooo... I took a book and squashed it flat! Anyway, I also HATE cooked mushrooms, they taste so slimy and gross. My favorite movies are the Harry Potter movies and Parent Trap.

When I leave school I want to be an illustrator for children's books. I would love a dog or a pet of my own when I grow up.

I look forward to hearing back from you and about your life.

My best wishes,

Ella

Letter 2 - Maureen to Ella

Dear Ella,

I was delighted to receive your letter and I hope I do not disappoint you when you learn that I am eighty-one years old. I have been acting on radio, TV and stage since the age of four years but recently I decided that enough was enough and now I only appear in an occasional concert.

I have appeared - a few years go - in the 'New' Broughton High, in a musical where the cast all were farmyard animals - I played 'The Queen of the Ducks' - it was great fun and the costumes were wonderful.

Previous to this I was in the 'Even Older' Broughton as the wicked stepmother in Into The Woods at the Fringe 1992. I have been fortunate to take part in fifty-seven Fringe shows - as well as working as an accountant - well very few actors can exist on theatrical appearances but you will find the few - who are 'stars'! I was fortunate to have a husband who was a playwright and he wrote six plays for me - including one that gained him a "Fringe First" - a wonderful accolade. He died six years ago and his plays are still performed all over Scotland. I emphasise Scotland because he loved the Scottish language and it was wonderful to hear the audience shriek with laughter at the use of the old Scottish words and phrases.

I HATE SPIDERS!! I have a huge scar where one bit me xxx

Kind regards,

Maureen

....

Letter 3 - Ella to Maureen

Dear Maureen,

It's really weird but my mum is called Maureen! I am not disappointed that you are eighty-one. I was soooo excited to get your letter because it nearly got lost!

I enjoyed hearing that you were an actress, I wish I could travel back in time to watch you act and meet your younger self. What was it like being an actress and getting up on stage and seeing all those eyes on you? Did you ever fall or mess up? If so, what happened? What was the story behind the spider bite? Was it poisonous?

I love Christmas, giving/getting presents, eating Christmas food and spending time with family. What is Christmas like for you? For me a Christmas is spent at my granny's house with my family.

If you could give some advice to a younger you, what would it be?

When my granny was my age, she was living in a time of war, when she had to be evacuated but she would not leave, she stayed in her house while bombs were going off. Do you have any stories or experiences of the war?

Yours sincerely

Ella

....

Letter 4 - Maureen to Ella

Dear Ella,

It was so very nice to receive your letter. I think I must have quite a lot in common with your granny. In the war, my beloved brother and I were supposed to be evacuated to Galashiels to live with our grandmother but we refused to leave our Mum & Dad and I can remember when the German planes flew across Edinburgh. My brother Joe and I got into our parents' bed and they lay on top of us to protect us. We felt very safe.

My mum and dad worked very hard during the war as they had a grocer shop, a bakery, a wee library and a sweetie shop. They would let Joe and I have our sweet coupons on a Sunday and we always chose "Dairy Toffee" because it lasted longest.

I had dancing lessons as "Madame Ada's School of Dancing" from the age of four until fifteen and was very proud to gain honours in Tap, Ballet. I was never very good at sports except hockey and I loved going down to Warriston on a Saturday morning to play.

I joined St Stephen's Church drama group when I was fourteen - only because my friends were members and I didn't want to be left out. The first time I had an audition I was cast as the wife of a sixty-five year old man (I was fourteen and even then we had difficulty in getting male members). The director was Campbell White, a very clever and talented publisher. He offered to sponsor me at London Drama College but my father was not happy and so I had to decline - this would have started me on the ladder and given me a good start - but then I may not have met the love of my life - Alan Cochrane. Alan & I met in 1958 and we did plays, pantos, musicals, after-dinner speaking and films - and always - together - so many theatre marriages fall apart without holding on to the most important things in life.

Alan died six years ago and I miss him every day. I always say "He made me laugh every day of our marriage." Not many people are lucky enough to say that!

I watch a lot of TV and read and I am a life member of Edinburgh People's Theatre and they still do four or five shows every year - this year it is panto Little Red

Riding Hood up at Church Hill Theatre and I'm sure it will be fun.

Yes - the spider was poisonous! If you ever meet up with me I will show you the large scar!!

Mess up!?!? Oh yes! Many times - but I always managed to say my lines and the advice my mother gave me was "THE BEST BEAUTY TREATMENT - IS - A - SMILE!"

REMEMBER THAT!!

Maureen

....

Letter 5 - Ella to Maureen

Dear Maureen,

Hearing from you is always the best part of my week!

I can't possibly imagine being in the middle of war and have to leave my family, I just wouldn't do it but it would be better than being blown up. In P7 we learnt about how people were affected by evacuation, rationing and the axis and allies. We even made a short movie using iPads, about a family being evacuated and I was the mum.

One thing i would love to experience is walking down an old cobbled lane and eating TOFFEE from that sweet shop.

I love to listen to the Famous Five because it's set in the past and they use lots of old and interesting words that we don't use anymore, I have listened to more than twenty of the audiobooks. I do not like the idea of actually reading but when I do read I go straight into the book and what the characters are feeling. I have never finished a whole book. What are your favorite books? I love watching movies, my top favorite movies are Parent Trap, Bridge To Terabithia, Home Alone, ALL of the Harry Potter movies, Mission Impossible and Mean Girls. What are your favorite movies?

Yours sincerely,

Ella

Derek & Norman

Letter 1 - Derek to Norman

Dear VIP,

My name is Derek and I am twelve years old, soon to be thirteen. I was born in Toronto, Canada in February which means I am one of the youngest in my year.

I was born in Canada then went to Spain, then went back to Canada, then I went back to Spain and then I came here (with my mom and brother). I got here in 2015, one day in September so that means that I've been here for at least three years and I speak Spanish too because I grew up in Spain. I stayed at Spain for eight years in total.

The things I like most are: football, F1, PE, iPhone 7, Fifa 18/19, FC Barcelona, Manchester United and Lewis Hamilton the F1 driver.

And I want to be either an F1 driver OR a footballer when I'm older.

Tell more about you?

For example what was it like in school when you were my age?

What was your first job?

What you wanted to do when you were a kid?

What you ended up being when you were older?

Looking forward to hear from you ;)

Best wishes,

Derek

Dear Derek,

Thank you for your interesting letter.

I was born on September 1939 in Aberdeen just at the beginning of the war. Later my Mum and I moved to Peterhead (my father was in North Africa) and went to school at the early age of four in 1943.

School was very basic. We did not get paper to write on because of war shortages. Instead we were issued with a piece of slate with wood around the edges.

When the teacher came into the classroom we all had to stand up.

The teacher had a blackboard.

We returned to Aberdeen when the war ended. My father returned safely. When I reached your age I sat and passed my Eleven-Plus exams (your mum will explain).

I went to Aberdeen Grammar School, a boys-only school, leaving at fifteen to become an apprentice compositor, a fancy name for a printer. When I was your age I wanted to join the Army but when eligible my father disapproved. Upon finishing my six year apprenticeship, I emigrated to Canada and got a job with the Toronto Star newspaper which at that time was on King Street. This was 1961. I know Toronto well.

After four years I moved to Montreal to a new job as crew scheduling officer with Air Canada. Then in 1972 returned to Scotland.

My last job before retiring was a Senior Guide at Edinburgh Castle, responsible for the security of the Crown Jewels of Scotland.

On my retirement in July 2000 I was invited to Buckingham Palace to receive an MBE from the Queen. A great honour.

In your next letter I would like to know your plans and hopes for your future career.

Hoping to hear from you.

Norman, MBE.

Dear Norman,

That letter was very interesting! Thank you for it as well.

So as you might have read I was born in Toronto and then I came back later, and those one or two years in Canada were AMAZING! And I was only seven when I arrived in Canada and eight when I left.

I lived somewhere around Parkdale or something and I went to a Primary School that was right behind the building I lived in and the playground was big and I was like the tallest kid in my class. So of course I don't remember everything but I do miss the place a lot.

My Future:

When I grow up I want to be a footballer or an Formula 1 driver.

Right now I play a lot of football outside of school and I go to a club as well and I will soon- maybe around January- have like a small six week trial training with the Hearts Junior team and if I'm good enough and I work hard I could get the chance to be in the team :)

F1: the reason why love Formula 1 racing is because of my dad. I've been watching it since I was two years old and now I love it. But it's almost too late for me to try and become an F1 driver because if you want to be a racing driver you usually have to start at a very young age.

FOOTBALL: at the moment I don't play for a team and as I said earlier on in the letter me and my football club will get the chance to play with the Hearts Junior team but I do still play football outside of school and I think I am a decent player and the positions I play are striker, midfield and defender and I think that I would have a good chance to prove myself!

Would you have any advice?

Yours sincerely,

Derek

Callum & Donald

Letter 1: Callum to Donald

Hello,

My name is Callum. I am thirteen years old and I am a boy from Edinburgh.

I like to cook in my spare time. I find it very fun and I also like to do sports, the sports I like to do is running (jogging). My favourite thing to cook is things with pasta, for example spaghetti bolognese and macaroni cheese.

My favourite place is Greece. It is extremely hot and there are many things to do there, it is super fun. And I also like going out with my friends at the weekend.

And I also want to find stuff out about you.

What is your favourite thing to do?

Did you have any pets as a kid? I have two cats called Pip and Pop, I have had them since I was four years old and they are both black and white.

I like to go to the cinema with my friends, it is very fun. What do you like to do for fun or when you were a kid?

Where are you from and what did to eat when you were growing up?

Did you have children, were you married, or are you married?

What was your favorite thing when you were growing up?

I hope you enjoy reading my letter.

From Callum!!!! :)

Letter 2: Donald to Callum

Dear Callum,

I certainly did enjoy reading your letter. You do a lot of interesting things.

I'm impressed by your cooking and share your taste for pasta. I also very much like Greece and Greek food.

I also share your keenness for the cinema. Today's stars are much better actors than the old Hollywood ones. My favourite was Clint Eastwood who can really act, unlike John Wayne or Gary Cooper. My favourite Hollywood films are East of Eden with James Dean, and Some Like It Hot with Tony Curtis and Marilyn Monroe.

You're a better sportsman than I ever was. My favourite sporting activity was always swimming. I was the worst second row rugby forward in the history of my school, which is why I don't like spectator sports.

I was born in Dunfermline, but we moved to Edinburgh in 1946, when I was six years old. I'm a retired journalist.

I'm a widower with a son and a daughter.

When I was your age I loved to go swimming at Glenogle Baths or at Portobello Swimming pool in summer (it's no longer there).

I went to the library a lot and loved to read, especially Sherlock Holmes and Robert Louis Stevenson. I still re-read 'Treasure Island' and Kidnapped. I was brought up on Brandon Street near where Stevenson was born and went to school, and I feel I almost know him personally.

As I grew older I loved to travel and couldn't wait to get to France and Germany. I studied languages and became a foreign correspondent with Reuters News Agency. A news agency supplies news from all over the world to newspapers and radio and TV. I was a correspondent in Bonn, Brussels, Moscow and East Berlin. I speak French, German, Russian and Italian. Now I'm at last trying to learn my father's first language, which was Gaelic.

I also spent fifteen years in Paris working for the French news agency. Now I'm back, retired, in my old home, Edinburgh.

I never had a pet, though I love both cats and dogs.

The other thing I did a lot and still do: I daydream. Dreams, including daydreams. One of my hobbies is writing fiction and dreams, fantasies and a lively imagination are useful things to develop the mind, even if one is not writing as a hobby. I always encouraged my bairns to use their imagination, to aim high, because I've always believed you can achieve anything if you try hard enough.

I'm still learning languages and I love travelling around Scotland, especially the Highlands, and re-discovering Edinburgh and its history.

So that's my story. I've loved my job and I feel I got a lot out of life with the joy I did.

My diet as a youngster?

Breakfast - Porridge, ham and eggs

Lunch - Fish or mince and potatoes.

Tea - Buns, my Grannie's scones, or a jeely piece and cakes.

It was great to hear from you Callum.

I wish you the best of luck,

Donald

....

Letter 3 - Callum to Donald

Dear Donald,

I found your letter really interesting, especially that you were a journalist.

When I was reading your letter, I thought it said you were kidnapped but i read it again and your favorite book is Kidnapped.

My favorite book is Diary of a Wimpy Kid. I like the whole series. I have never read Kidnapped before but I may read it in the future.

If you have given yourself any advice when you were my age what would your advice be and why?

I think your diet as a child is very funny.

Yours sincerely,

Callum

....

Letter 4 - Donald to Callum

Dear Callum,

Thank you for your latest letter.

Yes, my diet back then was also not very healthy! I share your pleasure in pasta and spent a year in Bologna in Italy during which I developed a passion for Italian cuisine - Bologna has a particular reputation for its cuisine. Its speciality is tagliatelle.

For further reading you might wish to visit the young people's section at the Central Library on George IV Bridge. They have a good selection of books, fiction and nonfiction, for people your age, not only Stevenson but a whole range of interesting books.

Have you a plan for what you want to do when you leave school?

At your age I didn't know what I wanted to be. But in school I started a wall newspaper in my first year when I was thirteen. So perhaps unconsciously, I was already heading towards journalism. I also had a talent for drawing and drew cartoons for the wall newspaper. I've often thought since it would be fun to earn my living as a cartoonist for a newspaper.

I didn't think much about the future except for exams. I was always scared of having to repeat a year so when exam time came my old Grannie would say to me,

"Jist pit yer mind tae it and say I'm gonnae DAE it! I'm gonnae dae it!"

And you know, it worked! I did it and since then I've always believed there's nothing you can't do if you put your mind to it.

I always believed in setting my sights high and I told my son and daughter always to aim high. I always wanted to encourage them to fulfill their dreams.

What else did I do at your age? I went on holiday to stay with an aunt and uncle in Kirkcaldy. My great pleasure was the dodgems at the Links Market in Kirkcaldy. Or bathing at Ravenscraig Sands nearby.

And the pictures! The Rialto on the High Street in Kirkcaldy. I was in love with Doris Day - a big star. But don't give away my secret. Especially as I deserted her and started to see French films at the Cameo at Tollcross and fell madly in love with French star called Danielle Darrieux.

Ah youth!

Look forward to hearing from you again.

Orrabest,

Donald

Dear Donald,

Ravenscraig Castle is very cool. It looks phenomenal, I have never been there but it looks brilliant. Do you ever go back?

It is interesting that you are a journalist, to be honest I'm not that good at writing but I still do my best. Any advice? What type of journalist were you?

If I'm honest I am not sure what I want to do when I leave school. It might be something to do with cooking or an electrician. I really like food and electricity is really interesting. What did you want to do when you were a kid?

My teacher told me he would go to Ravenscraig Castle as a child and he said there is a enormous monkey puzzle tree in the middle of the park. Was it there when you were young?

I looked up Danielle Darrieux and she actually lived until she was one hundred years old and she died last year 1917-2017. What was your favourite film that she was in? I might check it out.

I really like to go to the cinema with my friends and go outside it is very fun. My favourite type of film is an action or comedy film. What is your favourite film?

Last summer I went to Blackpool in England and next year I am going to Turkey which will be very fun. Have you ever been? Any advice?

I have really enjoyed getting these letters, it makes Friday last period wayyyy more interesting. I hope I get a lot more!

Your sincerely,

Callum

....

Letter 6 - Donald to Callum

Dear Callum,

Thank you for your well laid-out letter. My youthful summers were actually spent on Ravenscraig Sands, which was Kirkaldy's Riviera.

You say you're not that good at writing. But I thought your latest letter especially was very well written.

Everybody can speak, Callum. Therefore everybody can write. Whether you wish to pursue writing depends on whether you are interested, or not.

I love writing. I spent ten years as a foreign correspondent with Reuters News

Agency with assignments in Bonn, Brussels, Moscow and East Berlin. I reported on politics, sport, accidents and human dramas, international relations during the Cold War, and others including theatre.

Later I worked in London for the BBC World Service, doing radio where I really discovered that "writing" is really speaking on to a page.

So, advice? I think you've made a good start. Your letter has neat, precise sentences, not too long or involved. As far as journalism is concerned, I notice that you ask me questions - an important part of journalism is asking questions, questions, questions, then using the answers to provide material for your story.

When I was your age I didn't know what I wanted to be. I was a bit of a dreamer, even up at university. If I had been really smart I would have been pursuing career opportunities while still at school, in addition to dreaming.

Don't stop dreaming, Callum. Dreaming is good. But combine it with checking, even while still at school, on possibilities for careers as a chef, or in the electrical industry. And don't give up on your dreams.

I see you already started journalistic research by looking up Danielle Darrieux. My favourite films with her are a French film of 1953 called The Earrings of Madame de... and a 1952 American film called Five Fingers, a spy film set in Turkey.

Which brings me neatly to your questions about Turkey. I've only been as far as Istanbul but it is easily the most magical, exotic city I have visited, with the possible exception of Jerusalem and (maybe) Venice. I do recommend Istanbul.

I share your taste for action and comedy films. My favourite action film is Bonnie and Clyde and my favourite comedy is Some Like it Hot.

Go for it Callum. Go now for whatever you want to do or be.

But don't forget to dream about your highest ambition.

Best wishes,

Donald

Caitlin & Geoff

Dear VIP,

My name is Caitlin, I am thirteen years old some of my family are from England, Shetland and Italy. I have got about eleven cousins (quite a lot from Shetland), six cousins from Edinburgh and none from Italy.

My hobbies are football. I play for Hutchison Vale. I used to play for Spartans and Hearts. Some of the other things I like doing is going out with friends and chilling out. What hobbies do you do?

Some of my main experiences are being in a Florence and the Machine music video and playing football for Hearts. I am really proud of this. Have you had any experiences that you are proud of?

The places I've been and holidays I've had are Tenerife, I have been there three or four times, and I have also been to Egypt and Lanzarote. I would love to go to New York City and Disneyland. Where have you been and where would you like to go?

My idols are probably Ariana Grande the singer and Cristiano Ronaldo the footballer because they're good at the things they do. Do you have any idols?

I have a cat called Belle. Do you have any pets?

Anyway I am going to tell you more about my family, my mum is called Laura and my dad is called Robert. I have a younger brother who is three. His name is Murray and I have four grandparents and seven aunties and uncles. Please could you tell me about your family?

In the future I have always wanted to be a Primary School teacher because I used to always play it in my house when I was younger, or a lawyer. I also want to go to New York in my future!

I am looking forward to getting a letter back from you and hearing your news.

Best wishes,

Caitlin

....

Letter 2 - Geoff to Caitlin

Dear Caitlin,

Thank you for your letter,

I am eighty-six years old and of a very different generation from you.

I come from the north of Scotland from a small town called Forres. I did not belong to a large family and very few of them are still alive. I too used to play football when I was in school but changed to playing hockey and cricket when I left, however I still was interested in football and followed and supported Aberdeen.

I have travelled quite a lot during my life and have visited quite a few countries such as Australia, America, France, Spain, South Africa and West Africa, also the West Indies.

I am married and have one son called Sandy and a grandson called Logan. My wife is much younger than me and is still in full time work. She is called Linda. I did my National Service in the RAF and have had some varied jobs during my working life. I ended up being in a Sports Centre Multiplex with the Edinburgh Education Department.

When I was younger - a long time ago - I used to play the drums in a Scottish country dance band. So my taste in music is not really the same as yours. I have a dog as a pet. He is a West Highland Terrier and he is called Robbie, he is twelve years old and he is a very friendly dog who loves children.

I have been to New York and it is one of my favourite cities that I have visited. I still travel and my wife and I were in Majorca on holiday this year. Linda, my wife, is a Regional Sales Manager for a Luxury Cruise line and is going to Lapland before Christmas to attend a conference.

I admire your ambition to be a Primary School teacher and wish you every success in this. Stick in at school - don't get discouraged when things don't always go as well as they should.

I have two grand-nephews who play football for Hutchy Vale - their names are Robertson, maybe you have heard of them?

My own sport of hockey, I was lucky enough to be selected to play for Scotland in 1954 at Inverness.

Caitlin there is lots more I could write about myself but I won't bore you. I hope I have given you something to think about. Life is very different now to what it was when I was growing up.

If you care maybe we could discuss the difference in a future letter if you would care to do this and maybe we could discuss this some time.

I look forward to hearing from you and possibly meeting you.

Best regards to you,

Geoff

....

Letter 3 - Caitlin to Geoff

Dear Geoff,

Thanks for the letter!

You were saying something about discussing about the future.

So we should talk about that then. So in the future I want to visit places like New York and Disneyland. I also am curious about what I will end up working as and everything else that might happen in the future. What did you want to be when you grew up?

You were saying you support Aberdeen. I support Hearts. I see you used to play football and also you played hockey for Scotland and got asked to go to Inverness. That is cool!

Anyway I'm going to ask a few questions.

Did you enjoy hockey and did you get any medals or trophies?

When you went to New York was it good and what did you do there?

At the end of the letter you said there is lots more to write about yourself so tell me more!

Anyway that is the end of my letter I'm sorry it is a bit short. I hope I get a reply!

Kind regards,

Caitlin

Letter 4 - Geoff to Caitlin

Dear Caitlin,

Thank you for your reply to my letter. I gather that we may be meeting in the coming weeks. I look forward to that and how we can discuss how our lives have been different because of how the world has changed.

I did not have any specific plan about what I wanted to be when I grew up. Some things just seemed to fall into place. One of the things that I regret is that I did not pay more attention to my work in school. So a little piece of advice here: stick in and do your best!

My football finished when I left school but then I discovered hockey and I seemed to find it a natural sport for me, I played with some international players when I was in the RAF and afterwards I was fortunate enough to be selected to play for Scotland. I still have one or two trophies but over the years some have got lost.

In New York, my wife and I stayed in a hotel on the edge of Central Park and we went to see Strawberry Fields that the Beatles wrote about. Also went to Staten Island to see the Statue of Liberty and lots of other places.

I still live with my wife and our dog who is a West Highland Terrier called Robbie.

My wife is twenty-one years younger than me and is still working. She is Regional Sales Manager for a Cruise Line. My son is an IT Manager for a Business Company in Edinburgh. He is the first person in either of our families to go to University. He did not play football at all but he got into fencing and he got capped for Great Britain's Junior (U18) team.

I could write a lot about the different places I have visited in the world but we could possibly discuss this when we meet.

If you get the chance to travel grab it with both hands as it is one of the best experiences you can get and you will always remember the places you visit.

I am going to close now and I look forward to meeting you.

Keep well and kind regards,

Geoff

Brodie & David

Letter 1 - Brodie to David

Dear VIP,

My name is Brodie and I am thirteen years old. I like rugby, football, judo and golf. You might know some of my family like, because my grandma speaks to literally anyone. What sports do you like? I can guess that you probably have been in the Second World War, what was your part in the war? VIP were you evacuated? I like history and especially WWII so if it's okay in your letter can you talk about WWII?

WHERE are you from? Where did you grow up and do you like football? If you do I hope you are a Hibby because if you are we are off to a good start!

Last October I went to Turkey, it was fun and the weather was thunder and lightning but still roasting. Where have you been around the world? Where is your favourite place?

What was your job? When I am older I really want to join the army and be a paratrooper.

What is your favorite film? I don't really have one that is my favorite movie I just like soooo many!

Can't wait to hear from you, VIP.

Yours Sincerely,

Brodie

Letter 2 - David to Brodie

Hello Brodie,

To begin with I am eighty-seven years old and I was not in WWII but was conscripted in 1948 to do my two years National Service. I did eighteen months in Egypt on the Canal Zone as a Military Policeman dog handler and six months training in Woking, Surrey. After the army I got married in 1953 Boxing Day 26th December but unfortunately my wife passed away in September this year.

I worked as a driver for Parson Peebles at East Pilton for thirty-four years and the last ten years of my working life as a Lothian Bus driver. I was born in Caledonian Crescent, Dalry and went to Dalry School, then after the war moved to Stenhouse to a bigger house with my family.

My favourite film - I liked White Christmas with Bing Crosby. My wife and I liked to holiday in Spain, ie. Benidorm, ie. anywhere nice and sunny and warm. I enjoy football, mainly Hearts, but don't support anyone.

My time in Egypt Canal Zone was spent at No. 1 Dog Co, Port Said - Moascar - Suez patrolling the compounds at night with my dog on a lead, from dusk to dawn. Then fill out a report on the patrol for the Provost Marshal after seeing to the dog, ie. food and water and grooming each day.

Davie

....

Letter 3 - Brodie to Davie

Hi Davie,

Thanks for all the information I really enjoyed it. I find it so cool with your jobs. What did you like most about being a dog handler? What was your dog's name? Did you ever find anything exciting on your patrols? Did you like being a bus driver?

Davie if you were to be stranded on an island what would you bring with you to live with? For me the one at the top would be my Wi-Fi and TV to watch Hibs smash Hearts! AhAh.

Davie, how did you meet your wife cause I met my girlfriend in Primary School - and how long were you married? Me and my girlfriend have been going out for one year and six months. She is really nice.

You seem to know quite a lot about dogs and looking after them. If I was to get a dog, what type should I get? I think pugs are really cool.

Davie, what advice would you give someone my age? It seems you've done loads and seen the world. If you could give your younger self any advice, what would it be?

I look forward to hearing from you again, I really loved reading your letter.

Speak to you soon!

Your friend Brodie

....

Letter 4 – Davie to Brodie

Dear Brodie,

First and foremost: pay attention to your lessons and teacher as your state of education is what you will rely on for the rest of your life whether it is in your job or your everyday life, education is very important to you for your future.

Secondly I met my wife in February 1953 at a Old Tyme dance club run by her Mother at West Pilton Community Centre. We had a good relationship and married on Boxing Day 1953 and would be sixty-five years married on the coming Boxing Day. But like all good things come to an end, my wife Kathleen passed away on September this year and unfortunately we have no family but have plenty nieces and nephews in the family.

Now you ask about dogs for to give you an idea. We had one Tracker dog and six Barkers to look after. To go on patrol you took your tracker dog on a lead. But the Barkers were taken by truck to the area where the storage sheds were, opened the door and let one dog per shed loose overnight to guard the workhouse as the Egyptians heard the barking dogs which frightened them away from the sheds and so safe-guarded the property.

Hope to see you soon,

Davie

....

Dear Davie,

Thanks for the letter I enjoyed reading it and woowoo sixty-five years! I thought one year was long enough.

Sorry to hear your wife passed away this year. I can't imagine what that would feel like.

What was it like getting married on Boxing Day?

My normal Boxing Day consists of my jammies, my trackies, a turkey sandwich in one hand and a can of coke in the other. I can't even begin to think about having to even leave the house never mind getting married or going to a wedding! What was the day like? What was your favourite bit?

What were weddings like back then? Were they very different to now?

Your time in Egypt sounds amazing. I love that the guard dogs were called Barkers.

When you lived there, did you get to visit any of the pyramids? Or maybe the Sphinx?

If I could go anywhere in the world it would be New Zealand because I would want to see the rugby team play

From your good mate,

Brodie :) :)

Adam & Ian

Letter 1 - Adam to Ian

Dear VIP,

Hello my name is Adam, I am thirteen years old and I live in Edinburgh. My hobbies are playing video games and sometimes playing football - I have not done it a lot recently. I also enjoy going to the park and doing stuff with my friends.

I have blonde hair and blue eyes and I like to consider myself pretty tall for my age. I am Scottish and have been living in Edinburgh my whole life. My favourite food is chicken fajitas which i have grown a liking for just recently. My favourite football team is Hibs.

I was wondering if you could tell me what life was like when you were my age? I am pretty enthralled to know since I did not live back then and I know that life was obviously different.

I have another question: what do you do for fun like your hobbies and things to do in your spare time? I have another question: do you like football and if you do who is your favourite team? I have one more question: what nationality are you and where are you from? I would like to know since I think it is a interesting thing to know about someone.

Thank you for taking your time to read this, best of wishes to you hope to hear from you soon.

Adam

Hello Adam,

I have to say, I have never been called a VIP before, so that's a surprise!

So nice to hear from you. My name is Ian, and apart from a short stay in Kelso and Aberdeen, I too, have stayed in Edinburgh all my life. That, of course means my nationality is Scottish. I am nearly sixty-five. I have been married for forty-six years and I have three children, two boys and a girl. I also have six grandchildren and they keep me busy. I am now retired, and I was looking forward to have lots of spare time but I am as busy as ever. My wife and I help with her father, who was a successful boxing trainer, and his brother, her uncle. They both have dementia and are aged eighty-eight and eighty-four and require a lot of help and attention. I can't complain as they are so nice, and I'm sure it won't be long until I'm in their situation and need lots of support.

I am very interested in your life too Adam. It sounds fun. How many hours in a week do you play video games? I'm so happy to hear you go to the park with your friends. I still see some friends from my school days. I think having a group of close friends is important. It's essential to discuss any issue you have with people you trust. It's always good to talk about the things that concern you and not keep them bottled up. I suppose the best people to speak to are your parents or the people who look after you, though I remember at thirteen, I thought my parents were pretty uncool. Try and get back to the football though. You do feel better when you're fit.

I notice you typed you letter rather than wrote it by hand. I suspect maybe, like me, your handwriting is not so great. Sorry if I got that wrong. Nobody writes letters anymore but they used to. I tended to avoid it because it was not so easy for people to read my handwriting. I was also pretty bad at art. The big break came, for me, with the popularity of home computers. Suddenly I could write clearly, and send letters and notes that friends could understand. Not only that but I could design little things through apps I could download. I enrolled for a course at Telford College and got a SVQ (Merit) on Microsoft Publisher and I have produced a few magazines, (but not for profit). I was really chuffed with that. On reflection though, I should have worked on my handwriting to make people understand it, as it would have saved a lot of work!!! Is there something at school you feel you are not so good at, and is there something you excel at, and really like?

You were saying you like chicken fajitas. Sounds great. Although I wish I was a bit more adventurous at trying different foods. My biggest problem is I don't like spicy food. That cuts out so much choice for me. I tend to like more traditional food like steak pie, sausage and mash and haggis. I do like some Chinese and Italian food. I am trying to be healthy and cut down on red meat and now try to eat more chicken and fish. (I do love fish but hate the bones).

You asked what life was like at your age? Some things were just the same. Trying, and not succeeding, to be cool. Starting to take an interest in girls. (Who until recently were just a pain in the neck). Riding bikes. In the park with your friends, playing football. Supporting your football team. I think though, life was much simpler then. We didn't have social media. We didn't have to worry what the other kids were saying about you on Facebook. Everyone on Facebook wants to be perfect, and collect as many "likes" as they can get. Life just isn't like that. We all have our faults, and it's impossible to live up to the unreasonable assumption that we are all flawless. We had bullying back then, just as now. Back then, it was the big idiot throwing his weight about in the playground. I'm sure that still goes on but nowadays things seem to be more subtle. It's easy now to pick your target on your phone and slowly pull that person to bits without laying a finger on him or her. You might recover from bruises inflicted by a thug in time but this new way of psychological bullying can live with you for a lot longer. I wouldn't like to see that going on. Have you any experience of that Adam?

We are lucky to have, in my opinion, the two best football teams in Scotland here in Edinburgh. They are, of course, The Heart of Midlothian and The Heart of Midlothian Reserves!! Why on earth you would choose Hibernian, I'll never know. Joking aside, it's great you follow your team. Things can get quite heated when you're watching a game and that's understandable. There's a lot at stake. I never could, however, understand the hatred that goes on between some teams in Scotland. Whether it's sectarian (Catholic/Protestant) or just thugs out looking for a fight, it's just not in the true spirit of the game. When we were young, watching a game of football was the most important thing. So many of my friends went to see Hibs one week and Hearts the next. Changed days indeed. What's your thoughts Adam?

Finally, you asked what my hobbies are, and what I do in my (limited) spare time? Not as much as I used to. I used to go out with my friends cycling and did a bit of hill walking. I still walk with my friends on a Sunday but only for around two and a half hours. I still swim a bit. Most people look forward to retiring but as you get older, you start getting aches and pains and you find you have to slow down a bit. I used to read a lot, but to my shame, I don't manage to fit it in now. I try to do a wee bit of good, and I like to fit it around what I care about. My wife's brother died from Leukaemia around about your age. So every four weeks I go to the Blood Transfusion Department in Lauriston Place to give blood. I give what's called Apheresis, and it takes about an hour and a half. I have given around one hundred and forty donations. They take the platelets from the blood and these are used to treat Leukaemia and other ailments. As I mentioned earlier, we have two elderly relatives who have dementia. A condition that slowly takes away memory and eventually, body function. I now work voluntarily, two days a week at the LifeCare Centre in Stockbridge helping with a group of people with dementia and I really find my time there very rewarding.

You are still young, so maybe you have not given it much thought but have you any idea what you want to do when you leave school? Where do you think you will be in ten to fifteen years from now?

I hope I have not rambled on too much Adam. I don't want to bore you. I am looking forward to your next letter. I asked some questions that you could answer, or maybe tell me a little more about yourself.

We're coming into the colder weather now so keep warm.

Sending my best wishes,

Ian

....

Letter 3 - Adam to Ian

Hi Ian,

Nice to hear from you. I really enjoyed reading your letter - I learnt a lot about you for sure.

It's sad that you don't have a lot of time to do what you want but at least you're keeping busy and active. It's sad to hear about your wife's father. I hope that he is ok and keeps well. At least he is under good care, same with her uncle. You have quite a long marriage with your wife. It seems like a lot of dedication and it's just quite cool that you are married that long.

Now I'm going to answer some of your questions. So I am not quite sure how many hours I play video games a week but all I know is that I play a little bit more than I should but it is something that does keep me happy but I am thinking about cutting back some hours and maybe doing more studying since I feel I need it. And I can do more sports and yes try and get back into football. About the thing you said about me typing instead of writing you were right about my ability to write well my writing is pretty bad.

About the football thing, since I am not too interested in football as I used to I am not so competitive about the rivalry and don't really support Hibs just the team that I like the most but I understand other people's thoughts and opinions about it.

I also like fish - bones can be irritating but they don't mind me too much. I was wondering what is your favourite type of fish? My favourite is cod by a mile but I do also like haddock and mackerel. I do like all of the foods that you said you eat except from Chinese, I went off Chinese like 3 years ago but I would eat it if it was all that I could have that night.

It's interesting to learn what you did at my age and for Christmas I'm asking for a bike so I am really excited to go cycling around and it will be a good excuse for me to go out more. I don't really use any social media sights I just don't really think they're needed and there is just so many stupid things that I would just rather stay out of. I now just have a few questions for you just some random questions that I think would be interesting to know:

Have you ever left the UK? I haven't which I am pretty annoyed about and I hope soon I will. If you have, where have you been?

What is Aberdeen like? I have wanted to go to Aberdeen a few times but have no clue what it is like so I guess I should ask you.

My final question is what subjects did you like in school? Some of my favorites are PE, History and English.

Thank you for reading once again, I'm excited to see what you reply.

Adam

....

Letter 4 - Ian to Adam

Hi Adam,

Thank you so much for writing back to me. I was looking forward to your letter. Thank you for your concern regarding my wife's father and uncle. I really appreciate your thoughts.

You were saying playing your video game makes you happy. Anything that makes you happy is a good thing (as long as you don't over do it). As for you writing, keep at it and it will improve. We are lucky we have the option to use tablets and computers to help us these days. Use any tools you can to get what you want done.

I used to like English, Geography and History when I was at school. It's also good you intend to do a bit more studying. Anything that gets your brain going and stretches it a bit, will help your development and education. I feel now that I should have made more effort when I was at school. I know, looking back that I could have done a lot better, and that would have made my decisions on job and prospects so much easier. I found out later that once you start to enjoy learning, it actually becomes enjoyable and you want to find out more. In fact, your learning continues even after leaving school. Knowledge is power, and knowledge helps you make the right choices in life.

I think it's wonderful that you will try to keep a bit fitter and football is a great way to do that. And yes, try a few other sports, you might surprise yourself and find something else that might interest you. If you are lucky enough to get a bicycle for Christmas then, you're right, it's another way to exercise and, as a bonus, you'll get everywhere a lot quicker. You mentioned you don't really follow Hibs at the moment and that's just fine. Maybe you'll take a bigger interest when you are older. Or maybe you might like to learn more about the Hearts and support them instead! ;-)

You also said you don't get involved in social media. These sites can be very useful for keeping in touch with friends and sharing information but they also have a darker side. Maybe you are wise to steer clear of them for now. If you use them in the future always be careful.

As for fish, I do love cod the best. Salmon is also a favourite. I love the smell of kippers but the bone thing, for me, rules them out completely. You asked what I did for Christmas when I was your age. Some things never change. I wanted a bike. I got a few small toys and I used to get an annual. A selection box and a book or a record token (tokens were like vouchers to buy things). This was in the early 1960s and money was still tight in most people's budgets. Cost wasn't so important then, so we were quite happy.

Thank you for saying it's "quite cool" that I've been married for forty-six years. Maybe I've just been lucky, or maybe I just made the right choice. All through your life you will have to make choices. For instance, you are in the supermarket, and you choose chicken soup. Great. But when you get home you wished that you had chosen tomato. Big disappointment! Or is it? It's only soup. No big deal. However, when you have to make the important decisions in your life you have to take your time to be sure it's the right thing for you. Whether it's to do with your schooling, career, getting married, or having a baby, these are decisions that can affect your whole life. So choose wisely.

I liked working in Aberdeen, or the Granite City as it's known. The people are wonderful but some find it difficult to understand them, particularly if their accent is very strong. It's sometimes difficult due to the cost, and finding the time but you can easily get a bus to Aberdeen, have a good look around and be home again in the same day. Due to my advanced years, the Scottish government have issued me with an old age pensioners' bus pass, so it makes it easy for me to do those trips. I was told you could see the 'Northern Lights' in Aberdeen, but I never saw them. I also have never seen a wild red squirrel, or a puffin, but I was really excited to see a Kingfisher by the Water of Leith a few weeks ago. That was a first for me. So keep your eyes peeled when you are out and about.

Have I ever left the UK? I most certainly have. I love visiting new places and rarely return to them, as I want to see something new the next time I go on holiday. It's fascinating visiting different countries and seeing places I have read about in books or seen in films. I have to save hard to go but it's always worth it. I have visited most countries in Europe and St Petersburg in Russia. You said you liked history, well, all historic places you have learned about are here to explore and increase your knowledge. I have been to Egypt to see the pyramids and sailed down the Nile. I have been to North America, and down to Venezuela and flown over Angel Falls, the highest waterfall in the world. In Venezuela, I fished for piranha, spent a night in the rainforest and saw freshwater dolphins. What an adventure that was! They say travel broadens the mind. I can confirm it does, and if you ever get the chance, go for it. The rewards are immense. My wife and I are off on the 6th December to Budapest, the capital of Hungary. I can't wait.

I meant to ask, who is in your family? Do you have brothers and sisters? What about music? I am interested. As I was born so long ago, my influences are people like Buddy Holly and The Beatles. Who do you listen to? I guess you think, as I'm older, I don't listen to today's music. You're wrong. I like listening to Fred Shearing, Wrong Direction, Jay Zed and Raggy Boneman. I gotta keep up with the young ones, right?

I bet you're looking forward to the Christmas holidays and having a break from school. Anyway, get those fingers typing, as I'm looking forward to your next letter.

Take care and best wishes,

Ian

....

Letter 5 - Adam to Ian

Hi Ian,

Thanks for getting back to me I enjoyed reading your letter. I appreciate that you care about how much I study and my fitness. I feel it is important for me to do so. Right now I am not sure want to do when I leave school but I am thinking about doing something in history since I feel that is one of my strongest points but I am going to keep working hard to see if I can open any more doors of opportunity but for now I will make history my goal. What's your thoughts on that?

It seems like Christmas lists have changed about nowadays children ask for video games, phones, game consoles but I guess bikes haven't changed and some children still like books and toys but not as much as they used to. I am aware of choices you have to make in life and I am not quite sure if I want to have a baby when I get older but maybe in the future my mind will be made up.

I may go Aberdeen then when I can. If you do see the Northern Lights that would be a good sight.

I do hope that I will leave the UK and go somewhere like France or Italy. My dream destination is New York City - if i can go there in my lifetime it would be great.

Adam

Acigan & Marjory

Letter 1 - Acigan to Marjory

Hello my name is Acigan,

I am thirteen years old and I live in Scotland but I was born in Italy. I moved to Scotland five years ago, it was really cold when I first moved here. I live with my mum, dad, sisters and brothers. I really like English, Science, and HFT (Health Food Technology). I also enjoy writing, and drawing animals with pencil and colour it with pens. I also love watching on Netflix 'Thirteen Reasons Why' because people are trying to understand why a girl at school killed herself and I find it really interesting.

My one wish is to have all my family gather together and they can't come together because they all live in different countries. If we were all together, I would love to talk about what happened in the last years. I got one older brother that I don't really get on with but I get on with my sisters.

I really hope to be a fashion designer when I get older. I love creating things and making things because it's my favourite hobby. I help my mum to make a scarf and take flowers from my old clothes and made a nice colourful scarf.

School is nearly over for the holidays and the new year is coming up and I am going to get presents from my mum and money from my dad. I am also really excited about the holiday coming and I also like to go and watch the fireworks. My favourite colour of firework is pink, purple, and blue.

I would love to know who you live with and if you have children that help you to do things in the house.

I hope you have a really good day,

Acigan

Dear Acigan,

Lovely to hear from you, especially somebody your age! Thank you for writing.

I live in Edinburgh, which I like - especially how historic it is. Edinburgh was built by merchants and sailors and I love living so close to the sea. Have you always lived in Edinburgh since moving to Scotland? Do you like living so close to the coast?

I am the youngest of four children. My father was in the Foreign Office and was Inspector General of prisons in Burma. I grew up in Edinburgh but visited Burma sometimes. My mother was Australian-born.

I was born in 1929. The world has changed a lot since then and the world is a lot more accessible now, in some ways.

I don't use technology much. I don't have a smart phone - but I would be interested in finding out about how useful they can be and how they can help us understand other people.

I used to play tennis and hockey. Do you play any sport? Bodies are there to be used for the best means you can, so keep fit - it is very important.

Acigan, you should live life to the fullest and do your best to be a benefit to other people (if you can.)

I have a few questions:

How do you hope to live your life?

What would you like to give to life?

What sort of person would you like to be when you grow up?

What do you think of all this technology?

What is your favourite thing to do?

I would like to hear from you again, thanks for writing and hopefully meet you when I can!

With Love,
Marjory

Dear Marjory,

Thank you for writing great to hear from you too. I lived in Italy from when I was born and I moved to Edinburgh five years ago. I find Italy different from Edinburgh because it's warmer and summer is longer than winter. I have lived in Rome and I really like living beside the coast.

Wow your life seems so interesting! To have a phone it can be really helpful you can find things online when I don't understand something and no one is there to help me I use my phone.

Thank you for asking all these questions. When I grow up, I really want to be a fashion designer. I want to change people's lives by giving people free clothes and making the world a better place.

Have you ever been to Italy? Or have you ever been to a different country and if yes what's your favorite place you have been?

I hope you have a really happy Christmas and hope to see you after Christmas!

From Acigan

Dea Acigan,

Thank you very much for your letter - it's nice to hear from someone new and hear different points of view. It's important to try to understand other people better.

I have been to Italy, I loved it! I loved it because so much of European thought and history comes from Rome and Italy. I especially was interested in the art and music in Italy.

You asked me about my favourite place - every different place is unique and has a different and interesting history. I've been all around the world and each place adds unique knowledge - you should travel if you want to, and get the chance.

One of the places which struck me the most was probably Italy - it had a huge effect on me when I was younger.

It's nice that you want to help other people - I think adding to the world around you and understanding it is really important. Being aware of other people and what they value is difficult to do but worth it.

My advice for you would be to get the best out of yourself you can, push yourself and contribute back to other.

Acigan, I wish you a very happy Christmas and I hope we can both spread lots of goodness and happiness in the world.

Be the best you can and bring out the best in others!

With Love,

Marjory

Safiya & Tony

Letter 1 - Safiya to Tony

Dear VIP,

Hi my name is Safiya I'm thirteen years old and I'm female. Some of my hobbies are art, horse riding and I like annoying people with karaoke. I have been to Turkey, Malta, Germany, Morocco and Libya. Have you travelled much?

I'm not sure what I want to do yet. What did you do when you left school? I'm thinking about maybe work in a nursery.

I like travelling to Libya with my dad because I have lots of cousins there. Do you have a lot of cousins?

I am looking forward to hearing from you.

Yours sincerely,

Safiya

....

Letter 2 - Tony to Safiya

Hi Safiya,

This is your VIP friend Tony.

I enjoyed reading your letter and I have lots of hobbies like yourself.

I enjoy playing chess, playing walking football and hill walking.

My best achievement is climbing Ben Nevis in October 2017,

I also enjoy travelling and have been to many countries some of which are: Sri Lanka, Morocco, Mexico and going to Tunisia next year.

I do not have a lot of cousins.

When I left school I went to catering college to be a chef. I have been a chef for a very long time and worked all over the UK.

Look forward to your next letter.

Kind regards,

Tony

....

Letter 3 – Safiya to Tony

Hi Tony

It is nice to get your letter.

I have once played chess with my grandad it was quite challenging but fun at the same time.

What is your favourite football team? I like Hibs but I don't really follow it that much.

How was the view from Ben Nevis? How long did it take to get to the top?

I looked on the map at Sri Lanka, it is very far away. Was it fun there?

I would like to travel to Mexico. Do you know any nice places in Mexico to travel to?

Where would you like to travel to in the future? What kind of food do you cook? How many restaurant have you worked in?

My favourite food is a Libyan food called mb'atten. Have you ever tried Libyan food?

I am looking forward to your next letter can't wait to read your next one.

Yours sincerely,

Safiya

Hi Safiya,

Thanks for your letter, I enjoyed reading it.

My favourite football team is Manchester City as I am originally from Manchester.

The view from the top of Ben Nevis was very mistry so it was not very good. It took me four and a half hours to walk to the top of the mountain and three and a half hours to walk down!

It was a nice day (not too hot) and when you got half way up there was a lake and a waterfall. I now enjoy walking most weekends on the Pentland Hills. Have you been to the Pentland Hills?

Sri Lanka was a great holiday with plenty to see and do.

In Mexico I stayed in Cancun and Playa de Carmen. The places to visit are the Mayan Pyramids and Xcaret (which is a theme park). Do you like theme parks?

I would like to travel to Canada and Australia in the future. Where would you like to travel to in the future?

I cook all types of international cuisine. Do you do a lot of cooking? I have worked in five restaurants, four hotels, two casinos and now at the LifeCare Centre. Do you like to eat out at restaurants or cafes?

I have never tried Libyan food but I hope to one day. I really like to try new dishes.

Have you tried haggis yet and if so did you like? What do you want to do when you leave school?

Look forward to your next letter,

Yours sincerely,

Tony

Letter 5 - Safiya to Tony

Dear Tony,

Thank you for your letter I enjoyed reading it.

No I have never been to Pentland Hills. Is it nice at the hills? I would like to go and see them one day.

How was Playa De Carmen? Was it sunny there? I like theme parks but I don't like the roller coasters they are scary. Do you like roller coasters?

I do a lot of cooking but sometimes my mum kicks me out of the kitchen. What is your favourite food? I have tried haggis but it was very disgusting! I love vegetables.

Yours Sincerely,

Safiya

Reflections on Becoming a Pen Pal

Dear Super Power Agency,

It was very interesting reading the letters

Love from

Tasnim

....

These past few weeks have been pretty good and fun, better than what I expected and it was very nice to learn about my pen pal and how he knows Toronto very well, AND the fact that my pen pal has an MBE so thanks for you guys giving us this amazing opportunity.

Derek

....

I have enjoyed writing and learning about Ian's past and all the things he has done. I'm really looking forward to meeting him.

By Hilari

....

I loved working with you because it was very fun and it also helped improve my writing and I loved working with the volunteers because they are very helpful.

And it was good to work with someone who has a lot more knowledge and who is not the same age as me.

I am looking forward to meeting the VIPs next year.

Callum

....

My experience was very fun and exciting, thank you. I liked writing the letters it was very interesting. Out of the nine weeks, I liked learning about the person I was writing to. I am looking forward to seeing the books in the library and reading.

Femi

....

I really enjoyed having you at school every Friday. I wish it is a Friday every day so we can have you in the school cause it's more fun with you.

It was fun learning about an old person that I have never met.

It has been so funny there is never a Friday with the Super Power Agency that is boring.

Thanks Super Power Agency!

....

The experience has been fun and writing the letter to the VIP and getting one was really exciting.

And it will be very fun to meet them in person in 2019.

The best bit was not doing work in the classroom.

And it was fun working with the volunteers!

Have a wonderful Christmas

I have loved working with you, it's been fun writing to the VIPs. I enjoyed picking the title it's fun getting to write to an old people's home. Fun learning about an old person what they do in their time or what they are thinking and what their hobbies are. I would love to do it again. I can't wait to meet them in January. Gerald was the funniest person on the team it's funny seeing him every Friday.

Thank you so much,

Grace

....

At the start I thought this would be boring and difficult but I was very wrong. I have enjoyed every second of it from meeting the volunteers (they have been very very helpful) to writing to the VIPs which was a amazing experience, I have never thought I would have been so excited to get a piece of paper but I did.

....

I really enjoyed talking to my pen pal and I'm excited to meet them. It has been great working with the agency the lessons have been so fun. I would love to do more with the Super Power Agency. I now feel that I can write a good letter and I know that I will need that in my life.

Thank you for all the fun!

Caitlin :)

....

I have enjoyed writing to somebody new and I can't wait to meet them in January. I have also enjoyed learning about other people's life, it is very interesting.

Your sincerely,

Safiya

....

It has been fun working with you guys and working together as a team. We all had lots of fun together. I was writing to my pen pal and I hope to see them soon in real life. It was really fun and thank you guys for helping me write to my pen pal and staying as a marvellous team.

Yours sincerely,

Rakib

....

I enjoyed writing the letters I felt like they are actually talking to me, it doesn't feel like it's a just a letter. I was really happy learning about new people and how they're living.

Love,

from Acigan

....

I want to thank you for coming to Broughton High School, to our class with Mr Brown, our teacher, and working with us.

To be honest at first, when you guys told us what we were going to do I was a bit nervous that I was going to mess up. In the end I noticed it didn't matter how many times you made a mistake, it's actually writing the letter that counts.

I really enjoyed staying in contact with my pen pal and enjoying their stories.

It has been very interesting to be honest, I really enjoyed talking to Mary and learning more about her life and how it was when she grew up.

I was really excited to receive these letters because it's one of those things that interest me and it was as well really fun to write back.

I'm also really happy that I had a person to talk to, that had a interest in what I was saying.

I learnt that Mary loved trains and she went to school. I also learned she had a neighbour who had a dog, the dog loved cuddling into Mary. I was sorry to hear about her father that died while serving for our country

To be honest from my point of view I am really excited to meet Mary in real life. It will be exciting because, this is the person I have been talking to for the past six weeks. I can't wait to see what she looks like and finally be able to meet them.

This feels like a dream but it's not, it's reality.

Zander

....

It has been fun learning about what Charlie's life was when he was younger.

That he worked on a shipyard and sailed to Aberdour at the weekends with his family and I enjoyed writing back.

It will be fun to meet him next year so I can learn more about him after talking to him for weeks.

Kai

....

In January 2019 in the school library of Broughton High School, the pen pals finally had a chance to meet in person.

Reflections from the Big Meet

Adam / Ian

Ian

The letters were a very enjoyable experience. It was lovely getting to know Adam through this medium.

It was strange to realise how easy it was to work out Adam's personality from the letters.

I so enjoyed meeting up with him and found him to be a great lad with so much potential.

I wanted to do this as my handwriting is so bad so I understand only too well his difficulties.

I wish him well and am confident he will evolve into a well-rounded person whose writing will continue to improve.

Adam

I enjoyed the whole project. It was fun to write letters and express myself and learn about someone else and really learn what life was life back when they were young.

I was really nervous to meet Ian today as I felt I would stutter or just make a fool out of myself but I feel I did OK since it had been a while since we wrote and forgot a lot.

Ian made it good for me, he asked me a lot of questions and made me feel comfortable and non-pressured.

Overall I have had a really good experience and hope I can do something like this again.

....

Brodie / Davie

Davie

I am delighted to meet Brodie after writing to him. I am more than satisfied that the lad will do well in his future as he is so sure of himself at such a young age and I wish him the best for the future.

I hope that he continues in the manner that he speaks of to join the Forces. He is a remarkable young man and the future looks bright for him.

Brodie

Today it has been very nice to meet Davie. It's been good talking to someone older and wiser than me. I enjoyed how nice Davie is.

I was really nervous at the start and all about what he had done in the Army because I want to go to the army as well and I enjoyed his information on all of it.

This has been an amazing experience and we got to miss some class yassss!

....

Kai / Charlie

Charlie

It was good to meet my pen pal Kai. Surprise, surprise, he lives in the same street I was brought up in! Kai is into video games and he also enjoys a wide range of music. It has become clear as the day goes on he enjoys football, and tries to go to matches as much as possible. He is also keen to upgrade his video games as soon as possible.

We parted company and wished Kai all the best with his studies.

Kai

It has been fun meeting Charlie and learning more about him and what sort of instruments he has, a dog and two rabbits. He also used to live near the harbour, which is where I live now. Charlie also goes to watch Hearts playing football. He also really likes rugby.

Another fun fact was that he played the drums and moved it on a chair and played it like that. He also liked sailing to Aberdeen and played football in a team.

Danny

I have thoroughly enjoyed my time with Rakib.

It has been very instructive and has given me an insight into youngsters' thoughts in this day and age. Many thanks indeed for the opportunity.

Rakib

It has been really fun meeting with Danny. We have been talking a lot about school, education, etc.

We were asking each other a lot of questions.

We took pictures of our experience.

It has been very fun listening to what Danny says and also when he answered my questions.

....

Caitlin / Geoff

Geoff

Meeting Caitlin for the first time after exchanging letters was a very positive experience. My introduction was completely different from what I had expected.

This charming, articulate young girl came to greet me in a confident manner. She was not what I had expected and was for the time we had together a confident and charming young person.

Our exchange of questions was large and varied and a very honest dialogue emerged from then.

I would hope that Caitlin found the experience as positive as I have and has benefited from the exchange that we have had.

Not much more to say in regard to this but I hope I have contributed to Caitlin's experience.

Caitlin

Writing back and forth to Geoff has been really interesting and I have really enjoyed writing and learning different things about each other.

Meeting Geoff has been really nice and interesting. We have even ran out of questions, that's how long we have been chatting for!

Since we started writing to each other we have learnt loads. We learnt about family and the sports we have done in the past and now.

Meeting Geoff was really fun because we spoke way more than we did on the letters ad again it was obviously really nice to meet him in person.

....

Grace / Jan

Jan

The experience of letter writing and meeting a young person from Broughton High has been very interesting and positive.

It is an 'eye opener' to hear about the similarities and differences between being young in these days compared to when my generation was young.

The greatest difference is the need to rely on mobile phones and social media whereas in the past such things were in the realms of 'science fiction'.

It's good to hear about positive experiences at school and I was interested to know what classes are held these days and outings which are organised.

Grace

I loved meeting up with my pen pal and seeing them for the first time - it was fun. I liked writing letters back and forth to know what they do.

It was a really fun experience.

I like how this is getting put in a book and we got to name the book. Can't wait til the book is finished!

Thank you.

....

Derek / Norman

Derek

I thought my experience with my pen pal was very fun, it was something I won't forget for a long time.

It has improved my spelling, vocabulary and word use.

I have learned a lot of things from my pen pal.

If I had the opportunity to keep sending letters I would - it has been absolutely brilliant.

His best piece of advice was "Go for it. The only thing people can say is yes or no."

....

Oliver / Irene

Oliver

It has been fun.

Acknowledgements

We can't thank the pupils involved enough. Their engagement and the fun they had writing their letters gave the project an inspiring energy and it was all down to their drive and great attitude. It's a scary thing to write a letter to a stranger, so thanks for your bravery!

A huge thank you to our VIPs and those who support them. Bridging the gap between the two generations takes a special kind of person who is both interested and interesting - and our older pen pals were more than we could have ever asked for in that regard!

Many thanks to Susan Campbell-Dargie of LifeCare Edinburgh for helping source pen pals and being a great help to the project. Also thank you to Kayli Hight at LifeCare for helping with the Big Meet.

Thank you again to Mansfield Care and the wonderful Janet Love and Tia Dickman at Haugh House Care Home for helping source and support pen pals and making the project so enriching for our young people.

To everyone at Broughton High – thank you for always being so welcoming, full of energy and passionate about your pupils. Thanks to Rory Brown, Nicola Daniel, Moira Paton and Zoe Gillespie for all the help during the project and the Big Meet.

Thanks to our videographers who documented the Big Meet, Christopher and Stephen Cook. And thank you to our photographer Phoebe Grigor for the stunning portraits in this book.

The volunteers involved in this project were thoughful, supportive and the project could not have happened without them. Thank you to Jessica Armstrong, Jonathan Brown, Shiela Yarrow and Evangelina Sargeant for all your time and devotion.

Super Power Agency

Registered Charity SC046550

Find & Follow

superpoweragency.com

Instagram: SuperPowerAgency

Facebook: SuperPowerAgency

Twitter: SuperPow3

If you would like to volunteer with Super Power Agency, please contact:

volunteers@superpoweragency.com

or sign up now at superpoweragency.com/volunteer